NAUTICAL

Over 3,800 maritime terms defined

DICTIONARY

Harbor House Publishers, Inc., 221 Water Street, Boyne City, Michigan 49712
Manufactured in the United States of America

Library of Congress Cataloging-in-Publication Data.
O'Flynn, Joseph P., 1934-
Nautical Dictionary: over 3,800 maritime terms defined/Joseph P. O'Flynn.
p.   cm.
ISBN 0-937360-16-3: $9.95
1. Naval art and science—Dictionaries. I. Title.
U24.035 1992
623.8'03—dc20   92-34142

ACKNOWLEDGMENTS

I truly appreciate the advice of my father-in-law, Captain Walter L. Schick, the help of my wife Darlene, my son Jerry and my friends and co-workers Mike Perry, Hugh Pollock and Bobby Graham from Harbour Cove Marine Services, Inc., Somers Point, NJ

PREFACE

A number of years ago, my father-in-law, an "old salt", mentioned something to me about the "wheel" of his fishing vessel. Being uninformed in nautical terminology in those days, we had a rather confusing conversation. While I was talking about the steering wheel, he was talking about the propeller.

I must say that this conversation did create an interest on my part in nautical terms. After all, here I was a non-boater from a big city, living on the coast and newly married into a seafaring family.

In recent years, I have been involved in boat "brokerage" out of a local boat yard. Often, I see the same confused look I must have had when discussing the "wheel" with my father-in-law. After all, how many boaters actually know the meaning of terms like "short block", "scarf", or my all time favorite, "baggywrinkle"? Thus, I decided to write this nautical dictionary.

When I first started compiling the data, I quickly realized how many nautical words are falling into disuse. The trend away from wooden power and sailboats, plus technological advances, has caused this to happen. I decided to include these terms, however, since there are still a number of these vessels plying our coasts and an older generation of sailors still using them. Besides, it would be unfortunate if these terms should cease to be part of our nautical heritage.

Joseph P. O'Flynn
Somers Point, NJ
April, 1992

"A" bracket A strut often used to support the propeller shaft, shaped something like an inverted "A"

aback Position of sails when the wind presses their surface toward mast

abaft Toward stern

abaft the beam Direction of any object when it is more than 90 degrees from being dead ahead

abandon When all people leave a vessel while at sea, often in the face of danger

abate When the speed of the wind reduces

abeam Amidships, an object at right angles to the centerline of the boat; also called "broad on the beam"

able-bodied Denotes skill in seamanship

able seaman An experienced and qualified seaman

aboard On board vessel

about Go on opposite tack; also called "put about"

about ship Order, prepare to tack; also called "ready about"

aboveboard Above the deck

abovedeck Means on the deck, not actually higher than the deck

abox When the yards on one mast are braced in the opposite direction of the next mast, often allowing the vessel to be held in a stationary position

abreast When vessels are side by side

ABS (abbr) American Bureau of Shipping

absent The owner's absence on a vessel is indicated by flying a solid blue flag

ABYC (abbr) American Boat and Yacht Council

AC (abbr) Alternating Current (electrical)

accidental jibe Occurs when jibing or close to a jibe due to inattentive steering. Wind catches the back side of sail and throws the boom to other side of vessel. Can be quite dangerous

accumulator tank Reduces water system pulsation and prevents rapid on/off pump operation

acockbill 1. The position of an anchor hanging from the cathead 2. Position of yards when topped up at an angle to the deck

across the tide If during a windward tide, the wind is strong enough to hold a vessel's beam on to the tidal flow

ADF (abbr) Automatic direction finder

adjustable skeg A propeller shaft support which allows adjustment to the angle of the shaft

admeasure, admeasurement 1. To measure a vessel for documentation 2. Determination of a vessel's "tonnage"; also called "measurement"

admiralty law The law of the sea

admiralty pattern anchor Old type of anchor with a folding stock, plus fixed shank and arms

admiralty sweep When a small boat coming alongside approaches in a wide semi-circle

adrift Broken from moorings; "underway with no way on" means adrift

advance Distance traveled between when the helm is turned and the vessel fully responds

adze A cutting tool with a thin arced blade used to shape wood in boatbuilding

afloat 1. Borne by and/or on the water 2. At sea 3. Adrift

afore Forward

aft Near stern

aft cabin Rear sleeping accommodations

after Near the stern

afterdeck That part of the deck aft of midships

after end Stern of the vessel

afterguard Seaman stationed on the poop or afterpart to attend to the after sails

after-guy A guy may be called a "fore-guy" or an "after-guy" depending on its direction of pull

after leech Vertical edge of a squaresail to the leeward when a vessel is sailing close hauled

aftermost Object closest to the stern when comparing two or more similar objects such as masts

afterpart Part of the vessel towards the stern

after peak Bulkhead forming a storage area immediately forward of the transom

after rake A part of a hull jutting out at the stern

aftersails Sails on the mizzenmast and on the stays between the main and mizzenmasts

after swim Shaped underwater section of a hull which causes water to sweep into the propeller and rudder

aftmost Nearest to the stern

agonic line An imaginary line where magnetic and true north are the same

aground 1. Touching bottom 2. A vessel is stuck on the bottom

ahead In the direction of the vessel's bow

ahold Near the wind, such as to "lay a ship ahold"

ahoy Cry used to hail another vessel

ahull Vessel lies with sails furled and the helm lashed alee

aids to navigation Markers, buoys, beacons, electronic devices and other man-made items used by mariners to determine position or make a safe passage

air filter Filters particles from the air prior to the air being used for engine combustion. This helps reduce engine wear

alcohol stove Widely used since they are inexpensive and rather simple to operate. With proper installation and reasonable precautions they can be safe

alee Helm in opposite direction from which the wind blows

all aback All sails are aback

all ataunt Fully rigged, all masts and yards aloft, everything in good order

all hands Entire crew

all in the wind All the sails are shaking

all standing All the sails are set and functioning properly

aloft Above the deck

alongshore (often shortened to longshore) 1. Employed along the shore, such as a longshoreman 2. Living along a coast

alongside Any vessel laying beside another ship, wharf or pier

alow Below the decks

Alpha Used to indicate the letter "A"

alternating flashing light Navigation lights which flash alternating color

alternators Basic source of electrical power on a vessel is the engine's alternator. It keeps the battery charged. Older systems will have a generator which does the same thing

AM (abbr) Amplitude modulation; type of radio wave

American whipping A whipping in which the ends are brought up at the center and reef knotted

amidships Center of vessel

ammeter Measures electric current to the battery

amphibian Craft which will operate over the land and in the water

anchor Metal device designed to dig into the water's bottom in order to hold a vessel in place

at anchor *Said of a vessel when she rides by her anchor or is anchored*

bend a cable *Make fast to the anchor*

bruce anchor *Modern lightweight anchor, similar in appearance to a plow*

cast anchor *To let go an anchor, to keep a ship at rest*

cat an anchor *Hoist the anchor to the cathead and make it fast*

fisherman's anchor *Old type of anchor with a fixed shank, arms and stock*

fishing an anchor *Picking up an anchor by snagging it with another line*

flood anchor *An anchor used during a flood tide*

heave ho! *Cry of sailors when hoisting the anchor*

lie at anchor *Same as "at anchor"; a vessel when she rides by her anchor or is anchored*

ride at anchor *Same as "at anchor"; a vessel when she rides by her anchor or is anchored*

sea anchor *Open ended canvas cone used to slow the downwind drift of a boat in heavy weather and/or to keep the bow of the boat into the wind; also called a "drogue"*

anchorable Fit for anchorage

anchorage Designated area in which vessels may anchor. May be a protected body of water selected by the boater or it may be an area specifically designated by a governmental authority

anchor bell Warning bell which is rung when a vessel is at anchor

anchor bend Knot used to fasten an anchor line to an anchor

anchor buoy Small buoy attached to the anchor marking its position. The line to the buoy may be used for "tripping" a fouled anchor

anchor chocks Fittings on the deck used to securely stow an anchor when it is not in use

anchor comes home An anchor which has become dislodged and drags as the vessel drifts

anchor drag An anchor attached to a floating beam, restraining the swing of a vessel in a bad sea

anchor ground An area used for anchoring

anchor hold The hold of an anchor on the ground

anchoring The technique, the art of anchoring a vessel

anchorless Having no anchor, thus drifting; unstable

anchor light A 360 degree white light on sailboat masts used while anchoring at night

anchor lining Sheathing used to protect the sides of a vessel when weighing anchor

anchor pocket Shaped recess at the hawse pipe which allows the anchor to be be stored flush with the vessel's side

anchor ring Ring to which the cable is fastened

anchor rode Line used to hold a vessel fast to the anchor

anchor roller Fairlead over the side of the vessel through which the anchor line passes; also called "bow roller"

anchor tripper Device for casting off an anchor

anchor watch The "watch" while a vessel is anchored with specific attention to potential dragging of the anchor

anchor well Small recessed cockpit in the foreward deck with a hatch, used to store the anchor

anemometer Instrument that measures wind velocity

aneroid barometer Measures air pressure by mechanical means

angulated sails Triangular sail with the upper cloths parallel to the leech and the lower cloths parallel to the foot meeting at a girth band which runs perpendicular to the luff

answering pennant Used to acknowledge a signal under International Code

antifouling Bottom paint which repels barnacles

AP (abbr) "Advanced Piloting"; a course given by USPS

apeak When the cable is hove taut to bring the vessel over its' anchor

aport Towards the port side, "put the helm hard aport"

aportoise When the yards rest on the gunwale

apparel Equipment such as the sails and rigging of a vessel

apparent wind Direction and velocity of the wind relative to a moving vessel. This varies from the actual wind and is often indicated by telltales

apple stern Rounded stern with little or no centerline

apron Timber placed on top of the keel and running parallel with it in order to strengthen the keel; also called "keelson"

arched Said of a vessel, strained and drooping at each end; also called "hogged"

arm(s) 1. Lower part of anchor 2. extremities of a yard or boom

arming Piece of tallow put into the cavity of lead line

arse Lower end of a wood "block", which is a piece of wood with wheels used as a purchase

ashore When a vessel is aground near the shore; also called "stranded"

asleep A sail that is just filling and not flapping from lack of wind

aspect ratio Comparative length of the luff of a sail compared to the foot of a sail

astarboard On or toward the starboard side

astay Refers to the anchor line when it tends to follow the line of the fore stay

astern Toward the rear

at the dip When flags are only partially hoisted up a signal mast

at the helm When someone is at the controls of the vessel

ataunt Fully rigged

all ataunt Fully rigged, all masts and yards aloft, everything in good order

athwart Across; right angles to centerline

athwart hawse 1. Across the vessel's cable 2. Across the direction of the vessel's head 3. When a ship lies across the stem of another, may be in contact or close

athwartships Across the line of the vessel's keel

ATON Acronyn for Aids to Navigation

atrip "Aweigh," position of anchor when it is raised clear of the bottom

autopilot Automatic steering device

auxiliaries Sailboat with an auxiliary engine, considered motorboats when engines are being used

auxiliary engine When the engine is not the prime source of propulsion, such as a sailboat with an engine

auxiliary generators Provide 120 volt electricity normally for cooking, heating and air conditioning; also called "genset"

avast Stop

awash When the sea is washing over any item such as the deck of a vessel

away from the wind When a sailboat's bow moves downwind, a vessel changes course "away from the wind"

aweather Helm is put in direction from which wind blows

aweigh Position of anchor when raised clear of ground

awning Canvas over the deck which provides shade from the sun

awning lanyards Short lengths of rope used to secure the awning to the handrails and the like

aye Yes; also said, "aye, aye"

azimuth circle Rotating arm that fits over a compass which allows a compass reading while sighting on an object

BRAVO

B

back Reversing the vessel's motion and moving it astern by use of the engine or sails

back an anchor To place a smaller anchor ahead of the one on which the vessel rides to relieve some of the strain

back and fill To alternately back and fill sails

back a rope To add a preventer so as to reduce the strain on the line

back a sail Is to throw it "aback" (see aback)

back astern To reverse the manner in rowing a boat as to cause it to go astern

backboard A board across the stern of a boat against which the passengers can lean

backbone 1. Keel of the vessel 2. Fore and aft line supporting the middle of an awning

backing Wind changing direction, counter-clockwise in the northern hemisphere and clockwise in the southern hemisphere

backing block A block on the underside of a "through fastening" used to spread the stress and add strength

back rope The stay running from the end of the dolphin-striker to the vessel's bow

back sailing Wearing a vessel by backing the head sails; also called "boxhauling"

backset When a current runs opposite of the main body of water, an eddy or backwater

backsplice Splice, strands are reversed and interwoven to make a rope end

backspring Line from the dock to a forward cleat which will prevent forward motion of the vessel when docked

backstays "Standing rigging" from the mast to the stern of a sailboat

back-strapped Being forced to sail to the leeward due to winds or currents

back the oars Row backward

backwash The wash of a wave or backwater from a boat

back water Reverse the power or the push on the oars to make vessel go backwards

backwinding If a foresail is too tightly sheeted it may cause the wind to strike the leeward edge of the mainsail

baffle plates Plates placed inside a tank to prevent its contents from surging

baggywrinkle Chafing gear, on stay or shroud, made by wrapping with old rope yarns

bags A sail "bags" when the leech is taut and the canvas slack

bailing When water is dipped out of the boat by hand

baitwell A well, normally in the deck of the boat, in which live bait can live. Often will have a recirculating water pump to provide breathable water to the fish; also called "livewell"

balance To reef by taking it in at the peak

balanced When part of the rudder is forward of the axis on which it rotates, reduces the force necessary in turning the rudder

balance-reef Closest reef, makes sail triangular

bald-headed Schooner having no topmasts

ballast Weight placed in or on the hull to improve stability, may be internal or external, reduces "heeling" on a sailboat

in ballast Ship sailing without cargo, carrying only ballast

ballast fin Extension of the keel of a sailing vessel which acts as ballast

ballast line Vessel's water line when in ballast

ballast tanks Tanks on large vessels for fuel and water that can be pumped to various other tanks in order to trim the vessel

balloon jib Large triangular headsail

balloon sails Extra sails used in light weather when the wind is abaft the beam

balsa core Used to stiffen flexible panels in fiberglass construction by separating two panels thus producing a light, strong and stiff structure; also use "foam-core"

bandrol Swallow-tailed wind direction flag flown at masthead

bank 1. A seat running across a boat, a thwart, common in row boats 2. Ground bordering a watercourse which may be steep or flat 3. Bar or shoal in otherwise deep water

banking General term applied to cod fishing on the banks of Newfoundland

bar Bank or shoal

bar cleat Low "T" shaped device bolted to a deck or dock to which lines are made fast

bare boat Chartering a vessel without a crew

bare poles When vessel has no sail set

barge 1. Large double-banked boat used by a navy commander 2. Any flat bottomed vessel 3. Large flat bottomed boat which is normally towed and used to transport material such as coal or oil

bargee Person who manages a barge, a "bargeman"

bark Type of three masted vessel; also spelled "barque"

barnacle Shellfish often found on the bottom of vessels

barograph Instrument which continuously records atmospheric pressure

barometer Measures and displays atmospheric pressure

barometric pressure Pressure of the atmosphere normally read on a barometer which is used in determining possible weather changes

barque Type of three masted vessel; also spelled "bark"

barquentine Three masted ship with a square sail on the foremast only; also spelled or called "barkentine," "barque," "bark"

barrator One who engages in "barratry"

barratry Cheating or fraud by the shipmaster or mariners by which the owners or insurers of a vessel are injured

batten carvel Method used in building a wooden vessel when the fore and aft planks are butted together, flush on all edges and rove down on inside battens; also called "ribband carvel"

batten down Close all openings, fasten all loose gear

battens 1. Strips of wood put around hatches 2. Flexible strips of wood used in a sail to support the roach

battery Normally the source for all electrical power, usually lead-acid storage batteries

battery charger Converts 120 volt AC shore power into lower voltage DC to charge and prevent batteries from becoming discharged; also called "power converter"

battery isolator Prevents one battery from discharging into the other in a two battery system with only one alternator

battery selector switch Used when the boat has more than one battery in order to select one battery to be used at a time

bay A small body of water set off from a main body of water; an inlet of the sea

beach 1. The shore of a body of water 2. To run or drive ashore

beach break A wave that breaks near the shore

beachcomber 1. Long wave that curls up on the beach 2. A lazy seaman who loafs about seaports; more particularly applies to the vagabond white men found in the islands of the Pacific

beached Driven onto the shore

beachfront A strip of land that fronts a beach; also called shorefront

beachside Located on the beach

beacon 1. Buoy placed over a shoal to warn vessels of danger 2. A lighthouse

beak head Small deck built out over the bow of a vessel

beam 1. Greatest width of a vessel 2. Any of the main cross timbers which span the sides of a vessel horizontally and support the decks

before the beam Position of any object between directly forward and the beam

broad on the beam An object at right angles to the centerline of the boat; also called "abeam"

cat beam Longest beam of the vessel which terminates in the cathead and supports the anchor

on the beam In line with the beams, at right angles with the keel

spring beam The fore-and-aft timber uniting the outer ends of the paddle-box beams

beam ends When a vessel's decks are almost vertical due to her being thrown down by the wind and sea

beam knee Bracket that connects a beam to the knee

beam reach Apparent wind blowing at a right angle to boat

beams Timber stretching across a vessel to support the deck

beam sea Seas coming from either side of the boat

beamy Vessel with greater than normal width

bear Scouring block used in cleaning wooden decks

bear-a-hand Make haste

bearding Shaping wood into a curve; to bevel

bearding line Intersection of the side of the stem and the surface of the rabbet into which the planks are fitted

bear down Approach another vessel from the windward

bearers Non-structural members of a vessel which support other non-structural members such as the "engine bed"

bearing(s) 1. Direction of an object 2. Fittings which support a revolving shaft 3. Widest part of a vessel below the gunwale 4. Vessel's waterline when she is perfectly trimmed

take bearings Determine one's position by sightings with a compass

bear off To turn away from the wind

bears An object "bears" so and so in the direction from which a person is looking

bears off As a sailboat is steered further away from the wind

beating Sailing into the wind, with it as far ahead as possible; also called "on the wind", "to windward" or "close hauled"

beaufort scale Scale indicating force of the wind

becalm When a sailing vessel has no wind. Wind being intercepted by a vessel or land to the windward may "becalm" another vessel

becket Piece of rope placed to confine a spar

becket block Block with an eye beneath its tail to which the standing part or the tackle is taken

becket rowlock Piece of rope placed around the "thole pins" to confine an oar

becueing Method of anchoring by which the cable is made lightly lashed to the anchor's crown. In the event of "fouling", undo force will break the lashing and the anchor may be lifted by its crown

bedding compound Placed on the underside of a fitting where it is attached to the vessel in order to seal out moisture

bee block Small block with a hole through which a line is rove, often used on the side of spars

bees Pieces of plank bolted to outer end of bowsprit, to reeve the foretopmast stays through

beetle Wooden mallet used in caulking

before In front of

before the beam Position of any object between directly forward and the beam

before the mast A person who has sailed on a fully rigged ship and lived in the crew's quarters which would be forward of the foremast

before the wind Wind is coming from the aft

belay 1. Stop or cease 2. Make a line fast by turns around a pin or coil, without hitching or seizing it

belaying pin Vertical pin to which halyards are fastened

bell buoys Steel floats on which bells are mounted and operated by the sea's motion. Good in the day, night and especially in the fog

bells Strokes of a bell marking shipboard time, such as "eight bells"

belly band A strengthening band of canvas or other material on the sail

belly halyard Gaff halyard leading through a block at the middle of the gaff, normally part of the "peak halyard" on small vessels

below Beneath the deck

belting Heavy rubbing strip at the vessel's waterline

benches Fore and aft seats in a vessel

bend 1. A knot 2. To make fast

fisherman's bend A knot made by passing the end twice round a spar or through a ring and then back under both turns

bend a cable Make fast to the anchor

bend a sail Make fast to the spar

bend on To rig or prepare a sail to be hoisted

bends Strongest part of vessel's side, to which the beams, knees and foothooks are bolted

beneaped When a vessel is aground at the height of the spring tides; also called "neaped"

bent timbers Ribs of the vessel, the skeleton of a vessel; also called the "frame"

Bermuda rig Uses tall triangular jib-headed sails instead of gaff rig; also called "marconi" rig

berth 1. Place where vessel lies 2. A place to sit or sleep (also called bunks) 3. A billet on a ship

give a wide berth Keep a safe distance from some object or hazard

berthage 1. Place allotted to a vessel at a dock or in a harbor 2. Fees for dock or anchorage

berthed Vessel is docked

berthing 1. Exterior planking of the sides of a vessel above the sheerstrake; the bulwark 2. Act of placing a vessel in a berth or dock

best bower The larger of two bowers

between decks Space between decks

between wind and water That part of the vessel that is constantly covered and uncovered by wave action, most vulnerable area to decay

BIA (abbr) Boating Industries Association

bibbs Timber bolted to the hounds of a mast, supports the trestle-trees

bight Middle part of a line especially when formed into a loop

bilge Lowest point of vessel's interior, part near the keel of ship

bilge alarm(s) Warning alarm which may indicate explosive fumes or high water in the bilge

bilge blower Normally used to insure explosive fumes have not collected in the bilge, may also be used to control atmospheric conditions in the bilge

bilged When the vessel's bilge is "broken in"

bilge free An old nautical term for a cask or barrel

bilge keels Secondary external keels at the turn of the bilge which help reduce a vessel's roll, normally on larger round-bottom vessels; also called "rolling chock" or "cleat"

bilge keelson Longitudinal timber inside the vessel, over the frames along the bilge

bilge pump Pumps water accumulated in the bilge overboard

bilge water Water that collects in the bilge from leaks, rain, spray

bilgeways Timbers placed beneath the vessel when building or launching it; also called "launching-ways"

bill Point at the extremity of an anchor's fluke

billboard A ledge used with a "cathead" that supports the anchor

billage Same as bilge, the lowest point of vessel's interior, part near the keel of ship

billet Sailor's quarters aboard a vessel

billet-head 1. Simple carved work (not a figure-head), bending over and out at the prow of the vessel 2. A post in the bow of a whaleboat, around which the harpoon line is paid out

bill of stores A license from the custom house to permit stores required for a voyage to be carried on a merchant vessel without duty

billow A great wave or surge of the sea often accompanied by a strong wind

Bimini top Fixed or collapsible top that provides shade

binding The principal timbers used in building and giving stability to a vessel

binnacle Box near the helm which holds a magnetic compass

binocular Hand-held optical device with two separate lenses used to observe distant objects

bitt Strong post on deck to which an anchor or tow line is attached

bitter Extreme inboard end of a line, the inboard end of the anchor cable; also called "bitter-end"

bituminous paint Paint made from asphalt that remains elastic and waterproof, used on rigging and steelwork

black down Older term from when tar was used to paint the rigging from top to bottom

blackwall hitch A quick hitch used on a hook

blade Flat surface at the bottom of an oar

blankets A windward vessel "blankets" a leeward vessel's wind

blisters Domes over hatchways used to observe the deck without going outside

block A wooden or metal case enclosing one or more pulleys and having a hook, eye or strap by which it may be attached

> *cat block* Block which hoists the anchor to the cathead
>
> *fly block* A shifting pulley block
>
> *spring block* A common block connected to a ringbolt by a spiral spring. It is attached to the sheets, so as to give some elasticity and to assist in sailing

block and tackle Arrangement of pulleys for mechanical advantage, a purchase

block hanger Fitting placed around a spar in order to suspend a block in place

blooper sail Secondary running sail hoisted with the spinnaker

blow-boat Slang for a sail boat

blowing "Weather side" is the side upon which the wind is "blowing"

blows "Lee" is the direction toward which the wind "blows"

Blue Ensign Coast Guard Auxiliary Flag

bluenose Nova Scotian seaman and the design of their vessels

blue peter The "P" flag of the International Code of Signals

blue water Deep ocean water

bluff A vessel which is full and square forward, when the bow is broader and blunter than normal; also called "bluff bowed"

board 1. The stretch a vessel makes upon one tack, when she is beating 2. People boarding a vessel, "come aboard"

board a tack To pull down the tack of a course to the deck of the vessel

boarding ladder Temporary ladder lowered over the side

board sailers Small sailing craft whose hull resembles a surfboard; also called "sailboards"

boat Small vessel, no precise definition, smaller than a ship, most agree that it is smaller than 65 feet in length

boatable Navigable by boats

boatage Charge for carrying by boat

boat boom Outward rigged spar to which small boats may be fastened; also called "lower boom"

boat builder Builder of boats; a boatwright

boatel Waterside hotel/motel with docks serving those traveling by boat

boater A person who travels in a boat

boat hook A solid hook attached to a long staff with many uses such as snagging a line or fending off

boathouse Storehouse for boats sometimes while they are in the water

Boating Safety Hotline Toll-free access to safety information operated by the U.S. Coast Guard (800) 368-5647

boatmanship The management of a boat

boatmen Owner-operators of recreational craft; also may be called "yachtsmen" depending on the size of the boat, no established distinction on size of vessel

boat rope A rope to fasten a boat which is normally called a "painter"

boatswain Ship's officer who calls the crew to duty, variations include bos'n, bo's'n, bosun, bo'sun

boatswain's chair A swing type device used by sailors when working aloft. It is formed by a short board or fabric seat supported by ropes at each end

boatswain's mate An assistant to the boatswain

boatwright Boat carpenter or builder

boatyard Specific area in which vessels are built, repaired and stored

bobstays Used to confine the bowsprit to the stem or cutwater

bollard Strong vertical fitting to which mooring lines are attached

bollard cleat Twin "T" shaped cleat

bolsters Wood covered with canvas, placed on the trestle-trees, for eyes of the rigging to rest upon

bolt boat Strong boat that will survive a rough sea

boltrope Rope to which the edges of the sails are sewed in order to strengthen them

bolts Cylindrical metal devices, normally threaded, used to secure the different parts of a vessel

boltsprit Large, strong spar, projecting over the bow of a vessel; also called "bowsprit"

bone Foam that builds up at the bow of a vessel while underway

bone in the mouth Sailor's phrase for the foam that builds up at the bow of a vessel while underway

bonnet Additional piece of canvas attached to the foot of a jib by lacings

booby hatch Raised small hatch

boom Horizontal "spar" along the lower edge (foot) of a "fore-and-aft" sail

boom claw Similar to a "block hanger" but with four claws in order to spread the load more evenly

boom crutch Vertical support for the boom when not in use, has recessed area on top to hold the boom in place

boom gallows A span athwart the vessel with recesses to hold spare spars

boom horse A metal cap with a wide ring which is fastened over the end of a boom

boom irons Iron rings on the yards, through which the studdingsail booms traverse

boom scissors A collapsible support for a boom that is not in use, shaped like scissors

boom vang A system of fittings to hold the boom down under some sailing conditions

boomkin Short spar projecting from the stern to which a sheet block is secured for an overhanging boom

boot top or topping 1. The portion of the exterior hull at the waterline 2. A painted stripe at the waterline which is a special paint applied to the "boot-top" which is normally a contrasting color to the bottom's anti-fouling paint and the color of the "topsides"

bos'n's call Used for piping orders

bosun Petty Officer in charge of deck operations

bosun's chair Seat used to hoist a person aloft for repairs

bosun's locker Storage area for deck supplies

both sheets aft When a square-rigged ship is running dead ahead of the wind with both sheets of the square sails aft

bottle screw Another name for "turnbuckle"; also called "rigging screw"

bottom 1. Hull of the vessel below the waterline 2. Ground under a body of water

go to the bottom A wreck sinking out of sight

bottomry Mortgaging a vessel

bound Destination or condition of ship

bow Front end of the boat

broad on the port bow Direction midway between "dead ahead" and "abeam" on the port side

broad on the starboard bow Direction midway between "dead ahead" and "abeam" on the starboard side

by the head Stern of a vessel is higher in the water than her head, drawing the most water forward

down by the bow The vessel is too heavily loaded forward, same as "trims by the head"

trims by the head Vessel is too heavily loaded forward, same as "down by the bow"

bow and beam bearings Known direction to objects ashore

bow chocks Fittings near the stem of the vessel having jaws which act as fairleads for the anchor line and other lines

bowditch A printed reference work on navigation

bower Working anchor, cable bent and reeved through the hawse-hole

bower anchor Vessel's main anchor

bow eye 1. An eye bolt on which the head (eye) is removable from the bolt (pronounced as bow used by an archer) 2. Any type of bolt through the stem of a dingy (pronounced same as "bow" of boat)

bow fast Rope by which the bow of a vessel is secured

bowgrace Frame of timber used to protect the bows or sides of a vessel from injury; sort of a ship's fender

bow handle A fitting on the bow of a small boat used as a cleat and as a handle in lifting the boat

bowline Knot tied in a loop which will not slip

bow line Mooring line at the bow (not bowline)

bowline bird Span on the leech of the sail to which the bowline is toggled

bow oar Foremost oar used in a boat except a whaleboat where it is the second oar; also the person who pulls the oar

bow rails Same purpose as "life-lines" except they are waist high solid tubing

bow roller Fairlead over the side for the anchor line; also called "anchor roller"

bowse To pull hard and together, normally on the tackle

bowse away See bowse

bowsprit Large, strong spar, projecting over the bow of a vessel; also called "boltsprit"

bowsprit cap Metal fitting over the end of the bowsprit to which the forestay, bobstay and bowsprit shrouds are attached

bowsprit collars Metal collar around the bowsprit to which intermediate stays are connected in order to help support the bowsprit

bowsprit shrouds Stays providing lateral support to the bowsprit which run between the "bowsprit cap" and the sides of the vessel

box chronometer Ship's chronometer suspended on gimbals

boxhauling A method of changing from one tack to another; so called because the headyards are braced abox or sharp aback on the wind

boxing Kind of notched or scarfed diagonal joint used for connecting the stem to the keel

boxing the compass Naming the 32 points of the compass in their proper order

box off Turn the head of a vessel either way by bracing the headyards aback

box section mast Hollow mast built like a box

brace 1. Bring the yards to either side 2. A rope by which a yard is turned about

brace aback To brace in such a way as to lay the sails aback

brace about Turn the yards around for the opposite tack

brace a yard Trim the yard or shift it horizontally with a brace

brace by Brace the yards in contrary directions on the different masts so as to stop the vessel

brace in Lay yard nearer square

brace sharp Cause the yards to have the smallest possible angle with the keel

brace to To brace the head yards a little aback, in tacking or wearing

brace up To lay the yard more fore-and-aft

brackish Mixture of fresh and salt water

braided line Modern configuration of rope, single or double braid, has one braid inside of the other

brail One of the ropes passing through pulleys and used to haul up the foot and the leeches of a fore-and-aft sail, in preparation of furling

brail up a sail Haul in or fasten by the brails

brake Handle of a ship's pump

Bravo Used to indicate the letter "B"

break Place where the deck terminates such as the break of the quarterdeck or forecastle

break bulk To begin to unload

breaker 1. Small cask containing water 2. A wave cresting as it reaches shallow water

break ground Lift the anchor from the bottom

breaking strain Point at which any line or chain will break with undo force

break out To take an item from its proper storage place

break shear When the wind or current force on an anchored vessel the wrong way so that she does not lie well in keeping clear of the anchor

break tacks Changing from one tack to another

breakwater Embankments normally of stone or concrete used to create a harbor, most often not connected to the shore

bream Clear a ship's bottom of shells, growth and the like

breast band Safety band or rope passed around a man heaving the lead; also call "breast-rope"

breastfast Line used to confine a vessel broadside to a wharf, passes from the waist of the vessel, not the bow or stern; also called "breastline"

breasthook Triangular reinforcing member, used behind the stem in order to straighten the bow

breast line Line used to confine a vessel broadside to a wharf, passes from the waist of the vessel not from the bow or stern; also called "breastfast"

breast rail Top rail of the quarterdeck's breastwork

breast rope Safety band or rope passed around a man heaving the lead who may be "in chains"; also called "breast band"

breastwork Dividing or safety railing on a vessel

breech Outside angle of a knee-timber

breeze Wind of 4 to 31 mph

bridge Control center of the vessel

bridge deck Deck aft of, and separating the cabin from a cockpit, at main deck level

bridge eye Small fitting which is used in place of an eye, shaped like a half circle with flanges at each end for attachment

bridle Spans of rope attached to the leeches of square sails to which the bowlines are made fast

bridle-port Foremost port, used for stowing the anchors

brig A two masted square-rigged vessel

brigantine Two masted vessel, the fore mast is square rigged, the aft mast is fore and aft rigged

brightwork Polished metal and varnished wood

bring by the lee To incline so rapidly to the leeward of the course as to bring the lee side suddenly to the windward; and by laying the sails aback, exposes the vessel to capsizing

bring to Stopping a sailing vessel by bringing her head into the wind

Bristol-fashion Shipshape; clean; neat

broach To veer or yaw dangerously in a following sea so as to lie broad-side to the waves; also called "broach to" and "broaching"

broad on the beam An object at right angles to the centerline of the boat; also called "abeam"

broad on the port bow Direction midway between "dead ahead" and "abeam" on the port side

broad on the port quarter Direction midway between "dead astern" and "abeam" on the port side

broad on the starboard bow Direction midway between "dead ahead" and "abeam" on the starboard side

broad on the starboard quarter Direction midway between "dead astern" and "abeam" on the starboard side

broad reach Sailing with the apparent wind broad on the beam (quarter)

broadside Whole side of a vessel

broken-back When a vessel is so strained as to droop at each end

brow Temporary ramp between a vessel and a pier or wharf; also called "gangplank" and "gangway"

bruce anchor Modern light-weight anchor, similar in appearance to a plow

bucklers Blocks of wood made to fit in the hawse-holes

built mast Refers to a solid wood mast in which more than one piece of timber is spliced together; also called "made mast"

bulk Entire cargo when stowed

bulkhead line Line marking the limit into the water to which wharves may be built

bulkhead Walls

bull Small keg

bull dog grip An excellent temporary clamp for rigging, "U" shaped bolt with a shaped bridge which clamps down on wire

bull rope Line from the bowsprit to a mooring which is used to hold the mooring away from the vessel

bulls eye 1. Piece of thick glass inserted in the deck to let light in 2. A small piece of wood with a hole in the center through which a stay or rope may be reeved and with a groove around it for a strap

bulls eye fairlead Similar to a "bulls eye" (not the glass one) but has a base plate for attachment

bulwarks Raised side created when the "topsides" are carried substantially above the deck

bum boats Boats with provisions which lie alongside vessels while in port

bumpers Relatively soft objects placed between the boat and another object in order to protect the vessels topsides from damage; also called "fenders"

bumpkin A spar projecting from the stern of a vessel

bungee cord Elastic cord with many uses fastening objects around boats

bunk Bed, berth

bunt The middle of a sail

bunting Thin woolen stuff used to make flags

buntline hitch Simple hitch for attaching a halyard to a tackle

buntlines Ropes used for hauling up the body of a sail

buoy Floating markers

buoyage Series of buoys that indicate a channel or course for vessels

buoyancy Ability to float

buoy tender A vessel, most often Coast Guard, used to maintain navigational buoys

burdened vessel Boat which must "give way" to another vessel

burgee Small flag, pointed or swallowtail, normally used to denote membership in a yacht club or similar organization

burton A tackle, rove in a particular manner (see Spanish burton)

bus bar A bar, normally with attaching screws, used to make electrical power connections

bush Center piece of a wooden sheave in a block

busk To cruise or beat about; to cruise as a pirate

butt End of plank where it unites with the end of another plank

butterfly block Small snatch block with a long tail used for miscellaneous purposes on the vessel

butterfly ventilator Circular shaped ventilator

butt joint Where two planks meet and are joined close and flush with each other

butt strap A support plank bridging the connection between two planks butted together

buttocks Rear end of a vessel

button Ring on the upper part of the "leather" on an oar which prevents it from slipping outward

byland Point or peninsula

by the board When a vessel's masts fall over the side

by the head The vessel is drawing the most water forward, thus; the stern of a vessel is higher in the water than her head

by the lee Drifting so as to let the wind strike the wrong side of the sails

by the run 1. Let a vessel go without attempting to slack off 2. To let a line go totally, instead of gradually

by the stern Drawing the most water aft, stern of the vessel is lower than her head

by the wind Vessel is sailing as close into the wind as possible; also called "close hauled", "on the wind", "to windward" or "beating"

CHARLIE
C

cabin cruiser A motorboat with a deck and a deckhouse

cabins Interior of vessels if divided off by bulkheads and used for living and sleeping areas

cable Large, strong line used for mooring or towing

>**pay out** *To lessen the strain on a line and let it out slowly; also "ease" a line and "veer out" the cable*

>**serve the cable** *To bind it around with ropes, canvas or anything which will prevent it from being worn in the hawse*

>**slip the cable** *To let it run out end for end*

>**stopper a cable** *To put stoppers on a cable to prevent it from running out of the vessel when at anchor*

>**stream cable** *Hawser, smaller than the bower cable, to moor a ship in a place that is sheltered from the wind and heavy seas*

cabled Fastened with a cable

cable-laid Rope is laid with nine strands, against the sun (same as hawser-laid)

cable length A distance of 100 fathoms which equals 600 feet

cable locker Storage compartment for the anchor chain; also called "chain locker" and "rope locker"

cable shackle Shackle used to join lengths of cable, "U" shaped with a pin to close the open end

cable-tier Place in the hold where the cables are stowed

caboose House on deck used for cooking

caisson Floating gate of a drydock, when closed and filled with water, it seats and forms a watertight barrier

camber A curvature upwards. "Cambered" decks, tops of cabins and tops of deckhouses are arched to allow for better drainage

camber keeled Vessel with a slightly arched keel, but not hogged

cam cleat Made in various forms but basically a device that grips rope led through it with toothed cams that are spring loaded, often used on sailing vessels where lines have to be frequently adjusted

camels Large "sampson posts"

can Cylindrical buoy, usually green

canal A man-made waterway

>**stop gate** *A gate separating one section of a canal from another. Used to shut off a section should there be a break in the embankment*

can-hooks Slings with flat hooks, used to hoist barrels

canoe Lightly built open boat with a narrow beam and a shallow draft that is paddled

cant To tilt or slant

cant frames The timbers at the end of the vessel which rise obliquely from the keel

cant ribbon Decorative moulding on a vessel's side that sweeps upward at both ends

cant timbers One of the timbers at the end of the vessel which rise obliquely from the keel; plural would be "cant frames"

canvas 1. A general term for a sailboat's sails 2. A type of cloth from which sails are made but which has been generally replaced by synthetic materials

cap 1. Strong block of wood used to confine together the head of one mast and lower part of the next mast above it 2. A block of wood variously used 3. In older times a tarred canvas cover for the end of a rope

cape 1. Piece of land jutting out into and mostly surrounded by the sea 2. To keep the helm in a certain direction, such as she "capes northeast"

capsize Vessel lies on her side or turns over in the water

>**turn turtle** *To capsize*

capstan Machine used for heaving or hoisting with its drum on a vertical axis. If drum is on a horizontal axis it may be called a "windlass"

capstan-bars Heavy pieces of wood by which non-electrical capstans are worked

captain The officer in charge of a ship, informal name for owner-operator of a recreational vessel; also may be referred to as "skipper"

carbon dioxide A type of fire extinguisher

carbon monoxide alarm Warning alarm indicating poisonous carbon monoxide fumes from the engine are in the bilge

cardinal points The four main points of a compass

cardinal system of buoyage In this system, the characteristics of the buoys indicate the location of the danger in relation to the buoy using the cardinal points of a compass. Some nations use this system or a combination of this and the "lateral system"

careen 1. To lie over, when sailing on the wind 2. To lay a vessel on its side on the beach in order to clean the bottom

right a vessel Restore the vessel to an upright position after careening

carline knees Timbers lying across from the sides to a hatchway and supporting the deck

carlings Pieces of timber running between the beams

carrick bend 1. A kind of a knot 2. Windlass bits

carrick bitt One of the bitts which support the windlass

carry away/carries away 1. To break a spar or part a rope 2. When any part of the vessel's gear or equipment breaks or gives way

carry her way A vessel "carries her way" for the period of time after the propulsion method has stopped and until all movement ceases

carry on To carry all the sail possible

carvel When the fore and aft planks of the vessel's hull are laid against one another on edge, forming a smooth surface, not lapstrake; also called "carvel built"

case The inner planking of a diagonally planked vessel; see "cold moulded"

cast 1. Getting under way 2. On the tack on which the vessel is to start

cast anchor To let go an anchor, to keep a ship at rest

castaway One who is adrift on the sea or ashore

cast off 1. To let a line go 2. Undo mooring lines in preparation of departure

cast the lead Taking a sounding of the depth of the water with a lead line

cat Tackle used to hoist the anchor up to the cathead

catamaran Vessel with two equal size hulls held apart by structural members

cat an anchor Hoist the anchor to the cathead and make it fast

cat beam Longest beam of the vessel which terminates in the cathead and supports the anchor

cat block Block which hoists the anchor to the cathead

cat boat Boat with only a "mainsail" which can be gaff or marconi rigged

catch a crab To catch an oar in the water by feathering it too soon

catch-all Small sail, often called a "save-all"

cat davit Davit used to lift the anchor after it clears the water

catfall Rope used to hoist the anchor up to the cathead

cat-harpin An iron leg used to confine the upper part of the rigging to the mast

cathead Timbers projecting from a vessel's side, to which an anchor may be secured

cathedral hull A more complex shaped hull which provides good stability

cat hole Hole in the stern of a vessel for the play of the hawser

cat rig Rig consisting of a single mast far foreward carrying a single large sail attached to a boom

cat rigged Vessel having the sails and rigging of a catboat

cat's paw A type of a hitch made in rope which forms two eyes into which a tackle may be hooked

catwalks Narrow walkways on piers or on a vessel

caulk To fill a boat's seams with oakum

caulking iron Chisel-like instrument used in caulking vessels

cavil Piece of wood, bolted to a timber, used for belaying ropes; also called "kevel"

cavitation Turbulence caused by a propeller

cavitation plate Plate mounted above the propeller on an outboard motor which deflects the turbulent water from the propellers downward

ceiling Planking or other sheeting on the inside of the frames, along the side of the boat, not the overhead

celestial navigation Determining position by using a sextant to sight on various celestial bodies

centerboard Relatively thin board which can be lowered through the keel, used to counteract the tendency of a sailboat to move sideways

centerboard trunk Houses the centerboard and prevents water leakage since it extends above the waterline

centercase Watertight casing for a centerboard

center of buoyancy The mean center part of a vessel immersed in water; also called "center of displacement"

center of displacement The mean center part of a vessel immersed in water; also called "center of buoyancy"

certificate Government paper such as master's license

chafe To rub the surface

chafing gear Cloth, tape or material put on rigging and spars to prevent rubbing damage to the surface

chain Interlocking iron links used for anchor rodes

chain bolt Bolt which fastens the "chainplate" to a vessel's side

chain cable Anchor cable made from wrought iron

chain hook Claw type device which when lowered onto chain immediately stops its "pay out"; also called "devil's claw"

chain knot A succession of loops in a line with each loop being passed through the previous one, looks similar to a chain

chain locker Storage compartment for the anchor chain; also called "cable locker" and "rope locker"

in chains *Refers to an individual using the lead line while standing in the chain locker*

chain pipe Pipe through which the anchor chain passes

chainplates Iron bolted to side of ship to which chains and dead-eyes of the lower rigging are connected; also called "shroud plates" and "channel plates"

chain-wales Planks bolted edgewise to the outside of a vessel. Narrow vessels use them for spreading the lower rigging; also called "channels" and "channel-boards"

chamfer To bevel a plank

chandlery Shop selling nautical gear

channel Navigable portion of a waterway

channel boards Planks bolted edgewise to the outside of a vessel. Narrow vessels use them for spreading the lower rigging; also called "channels" and "chain-wales"

channel plates Iron bolted to side of ship, to which the chains and dead-eyes of the lower rigging are connected; also called "shroud plates" and "chainplates"

channels Planks bolted edgewise to the outside of a vessel. Narrow vessels use them for spreading the lower rigging; also called "chain-wales" and "channel-boards"

chapelling Unintentionally putting a close hauled vessel's bow into the wind and having to circle around until the course can be resumed

Charlie Used to indicate the letter "C"

charlie noble A stovepipe fitting in a cabin top

chart 1. To lay out a course 2. A seagoing map

charter 1. Lease a vessel on a temporary basis 2. The contract to lease such a vessel is called the "charter"

lay day A day allowed to a person chartering a vessel in which to load or unload cargo or belongings

charterer Person who charters vessels

chart house A cabin near the helm to store and use charts for navigation; also called "chart room"

chart information Recording information on an existing chart of the area

chart measurer A small navigation device with a small geared wheel, as the wheel is rolled across a chart it indicates distances

check To stop or impede

cheek block A sheave which has only one half of a shell, the half shell and the item to which it is attached hold the line and sheave in place

cheeks Sides of the shell of a block

cheese down Coiling a rope on the deck in an opposite way to the "Flemish coil"

chine When the bottom and the topsides of the vessel meet at a well-defined area rather than a gradual curve—this is the "chine" of the boat

chine log A longitudinal member used at the intersection of the sides and bottom of flat or V-bottom boats

chinse To drive oakum into seams

chinsing iron Small chisel used to chinse a vessel

chip The quadrant-shaped piece of wood attached to a log line of a "chip log"

chip log Older method of determining a vessel's speed by towing a specially designed board from the stern. Speed is determined by the amount of log line run out during a fixed period of time

chippy or chips Nickname for ship's carpenter

chisel scraper Long handled scraper used to remove barnacles

chock A "U" or "O" shaped fitting on the deck used to control rigging or mooring lines

chockablock When the upper and lower blocks are too close to hoist any higher; also called "two-blocks"

chocks 1. Deck fittings with inward curving arms through which lines are passed to lead them on or off the boat 2. Wedges used to secure something

chop 1. Confused water action found where tidal currents meet or closely spaced waves caused by the wind 2. The hulk of a boat remodeled for use as a residence

chopping Tumbling waves dashing against each other

choppy Small, rough and turbulent waves

christen To name or dedicate a ship at a ceremony

chronometer A very accurate timepiece

>*box chronometer Ship's chronometer suspended on gimbals*

circuit breaker A switch which automatically interrupts electrical current due to an abnormal condition, such as an overload, used in place of fuses

cistern An apartment in the hold, has a pipe to the outside with a seacock which may let water in

clack valve Valve hinged on one end which will open with suction or force and closes with a clacking sound

clamps Planks on the inside of the vessel to support the ends of the deck beams; also called "deck shelf"

clap on Make more sail; "clap on sail"

clapotic waves Waves caused by the sea hitting a high shoreline which returns them with some force into the incoming seas; can be very dangerous

clapper 1. The tongue of a bell 2. The chafing piece in the jaws of a gaff

classes Grouping of boats to equalize performance in racing

clawing off To work off close-hauled from the lee shore

clean lines When a boat's lines allow her to slip easily through the water

clear 1. Lines are "clear" when they run freely 2. To untangle and straighten out lines and rigging 3. Also used as clear customs, leave the shore, pass an obstacle safely, remove water from the bilge

clearance Certificate that a vessel has been "cleared" by customs to sail

cleat A fitting with "horns" on which lines can be fastened

>*bar cleat Low "T" shaped device bolted to a deck or dock to which lines are made fast*

>*bollard cleat Twin "T" shaped cleat*

cleat hitch Crisscross or figure eight hitch used to fasten a line to a cleat

clench or clinch 1. The part of the cable attached to the anchor ring 2. The knot used to fasten a cable to the anchor ring

clevis Link in chain with movable bolt so chain can be separated, used to connect anchor lines, fasten blocks, "shackle"

clevis pin Pin with a small head on one end and a hole for a split pin in the other end

clew Lower corner of square sails

clew coupling Two "U" bolts which screw together, used to connect a sheet to the clew of a headsail

clew garnet A tackle or rope and pulley fastened to the clews of the mainsail and foresail to truss them up to the yard

clew iron An iron loop with thimbles for use at the corner of a sail

clewline Rope that hauls up the clew of a square sail

clew up To finish something

clinch A half-hitch, stopped to its own part

clinch or clench 1. The part of the cable attached to the anchor ring 2. The knot used to fasten a cable to the anchor ring

clinker Lapstrake planking

clinometer Instrument with a graduated dial and a pendulum which indicates the angle of the vessel's heel

clip hooks Flat hooks that are designed to only connect with one another, used as a fast method to connect two lines

clipper Fast sailing vessel of the 19th century with long slender lines, an overhanging bow, tall raking masts and a large sail area

clipper bow A bow with a concave profile

clipper built Built along the lines of a "clipper" ship

clock (ship's) A clock which strikes one to eight bells every half hour along with the divisions of the ship's watches

clock calm Very calm weather

close aboard When a vessel passes close to an object "abeam"

closed base cleat A "T" shaped cleat with no hole in the base for a line

closed cooling Engine contains its own fresh water and/or coolant in order to cool the engine, the heat is then transferred to the outside water by a "heat exchanger" or "keel cooler"

close hauled Vessel is sailing as close into the wind as possible; also called "on the wind", "to windward" or "beating"

close jammed Sailing so close to the wind that any movement towards the wind puts the sails aback

close linked Small chains without studs across the widest part of each link

close reach A sailing vessel is on a "close reach" when the wind is just forward of the beam, but the vessel is not close-hauled

close reefed When all the reefs are taken in

close winded Vessel which can efficiently go to the windward

close with the land To approach the land

clove hitch Two half-hitches around a spar or piling

clove hook Iron clasps, in two parts, moving on the same pivot and overlapping

club Spar at the foot of a triangular headsail; also called "club boom"

clubbing Drifting down a current with an anchor out

club footed Vessel with a wide forefoot

clubhaul To tack by letting go the lee anchor as soon as the wind is out of the sails. This brings the vessel's head into the wind. As soon as the ca-ble pays off, it is cut and the sails are trimmed

club topsail Oversize gaff topsail using "clubs" to extend the mast and the gaff; also called "jackyard topsail"

clump block Heavy duty block with a larger than normal swallow

CME (abbr) Courtesy Motorboat Examination (Coast Guard Auxiliary)

CMG (abbr) Course Made Good

CNG (abbr) Compressed Natural Gas

CO (abbr) Carbon monoxide, poisonous gas

coach bolt Common bolt which may have various types of heads

coal tar Tar made from a bituminous substance

coaming boards Boards around the cockpit of smaller sail boats which help prevent splash from coming into the cockpit and provide a back rest for the cockpit's occupants

coaming bolster A pad for human comfort on a cockpit seat

coamings Raised work around the hatches which prevents water from getting into vessel

coast Land nearest the sea

coastal Pertaining to the coast

coastal tug boat Although often capable of operating over large areas, they are not normally deep draft vessels. This restricts them from safely being operated long distances from the shore. They will normally have twin propellers.

coast charts Fairly large scale chart showing a relatively limited area, used for close-in coastal navigation and entering of harbors

coaster 1. Sailing along the shore 2. Resident of the seacoast 3. Vessel employed in sailing along the coast 4. Vessel trading from port to port in the same country

Coast Guard, U.S. Federal marine law enforcement agency

coasting Sailing along or near the shore

coasting trade *Trade which is carried on between different ports of the same country*

coastland Land bordering on the sea

coast line Boundary between the sea or a lake and the land

Coast Pilots Reference books with helpful navigation information to be used in conjunction with nautical charts, issued by the U. S. National Ocean Service

coastward Toward the coast

coastwise Going along the coast

cock bill 1. The position of an anchor hanging from the cathead 2. The position of the yards when topped up at an angle to the deck; also called "acockbill"

cock boat A small ship's boat

cockpit Space or well, sunken into the deck

cockswain See coxswain which is currently the more popular spelling

code Any of several systems used to transmit messages

code signals Flag signals for speaking at sea

codline An eighteen thread line

cog A small boat; a small fishing boat

coil A quantity of rope laid in a circle

cold front Forward edge of a mass of cold air

cold molded Method of building a strong boat using various diagonal layers of light wood formed over a mould

collar An eye in the end of a shroud or stay, which goes over the masthead

collier Ship built for or used to carry coal

colors 1. Hoisting boat's flag at 8:00 a.m. 2. Flag(s) flown to indicate the vessel's nationality; commonly used to include all flags flown

colors are made The ceremonial raising of the flag at 8:00 a.m.

COLREGS (Acronym) Rules of the Road

combers Long curling waves

combing Another term for "coaming"

come aboard People boarding the vessel; also "board"

come about To tack; change direction in relation to the wind

come up the tackle fall Slacken the tackle gently

come up with the capstan Turn the capstan the contrary way

commission Making a ship ready for active use

companion Covering over the staircase to a cabin

companion hatch Sort of a porch placed over the ladder to a cabin

companion ladder Steps which lead down from the deck; also called "companionways"

company Ship's crew including officers

compartments Interior area divided off by bulkheads such as the "engine compartment"

compass Instrument showing course of the vessel

dumb compass *A "pelorus," which is a sighting device without a compass, used to determine relative bearing* *fetch a compass* Take a round about course

flinders bar Iron bar placed near a compass to reduce deviation caused by local influence

mariner's compass Compass used to navigate a vessel that has parallel magnetic needles or bundles of needles permanently attached to a card marked to indicate the direction and the degrees of a circle

points of the compass The thirty-two points of direction into which the compass card of a mariner's compass is divided

pole or masthead compass A compass elevated above the deck in order to minimize the effect of the ship's attraction

compass bowl Glass covered metal container of a mariner's compass

compass card Has a magnetic needle and floats on pivots inside of the compass

compass course Course steered by use of a compass

compass dial A compass card

compass error Results from "variation" and "deviation"

compass rose The compass card which is printed on charts

compass signal A signal showing a particular point of the compass

compass timber Any timber which is not straight

composite construction Use of more than one material in the hull of a vessel

compressed natural gas stove (CNG) Relatively new in use for shipboard cooking, safer than LPG

con Direct the course or the steering of a vessel

concrete boat Ferro-cement constructed vessel

confused sea Irregular sea coming from more than one direction; also called "cross sea"

conical buoy Buoy having a conical shape above the water

conning Directing the helmsman in the steering of a vessel

container vessel Large cargo vessel used to carry containers of cargo. Containers are designed not only to be readily shipped on vessels but to be carried by tractor trailers and railroad flat cars

continental fairlead Fairlead on which the horns are angled next to one another, the rope enters and is trapped easily; also called "skene chock"

control station The "bridge" or "control center" of a small vessel

copper punt A raft used by ship's personnel to paint the sides of a vessel near the waterline

cordage All rope and small line

Corinthian Amateur yachtsman; a non-professional in boating

counter After portion of a boat from the waterline to the extreme outward swell or stern overhang

counter-brace 1. Lee brace of the foretopsail yard 2. To brace the yards in opposite directions

countersink Normally refers to wood screws which have their heads sunk below the wood surface

counter-timbers Short timbers put in to strengthen the counter

course Direction a vessel is steered or a pre-arranged course to be followed in a race

courses Common term for the sails that hang from ship's lower yards

cow hitch A simple slip knot

cow tails Ends of a line which has unraveled

cowl ventilator Traditional type of ventilator of cylindrical shape with a flared top bent out at a 90 degree angle

coxswain Person who steers the boat

CQR "Secure" A patented anchor; also called a "plow anchor"

crab Drift sideways

cradle Framework that supports a boat while it is being hauled out on a "way" or when the boat is being stored on land

craft General term applied to any collection of small vessels

cranes Machine used for hoisting

crank A vessel which is inclined to lean over and cannot bear much sail, opposite of "stiff"

cranse iron Steel band or cap at the outer end of the bowsprit used to connect the stays

crazing Cobweb type small cracking that develops on old fiberglass gelcoat

creeper Iron instrument with four claws, used for dragging the bottom of a harbor

crew All the persons working on and responsible for the operation of any vessel

crew boat Normally, a boat used to transport a work force to a work site on the water, such as an oil rig

cringle A thimble, grommet, eyelet or rope loop at the edge of a sail and used for making rope and lines fast

crinolenes Lines connected to a purchase block used to steady a lifted item

cross Raise a yard to its proper position on a mast

crossbars Round bars of iron used to turn the shank of an anchor

crossbeam Timber binding the sides of a vessel

cross bearings Bearings taken of two different objects which when plotted on a chart indicate the vessel's position

cross bitt Piece of timber bolted across two bitts for a rope fastening

cross bollards A mooring bollard shaped like a cross

crosscurrent Current running counter to the general forward direction

crossing situation Passing in accordance with Navigation Rules

cross jack Lower yard in the mizzen mast

cross keelson Strong timber laid across the keelson to give support to heavy equipment and engines

cross pawl Timber that keeps the vessel together during building while just a frame

crosspiece 1. Rail extending over the windlass, furnished with pins to which rigging is fastened when required 2. A cross bitt

cross sea An irregular sea coming from more than one direction; also called "confused sea"

cross spales Timbers nailed across a vessel to the frames which hold the sides together until the knees are bolted

cross the line To cross the equator

crosstrees Timber secured to the mast athwartships, used to spread the the shrouds

crow's nest Observation platform set above the mast's cross trees

crow-foot Small lines rove through the euvrou to suspend an awning

crowd on To carry the maximum amount of sail

crowd sail Make the best speed by spreading all the sails

crown Place where the arms are joined to the shank of an anchor

crown a knot To pass the strands over and under each other above the knot. This is the first part of a backsplice in which the strands are reversed and interwoven to make a rope end

cruise To sail about stopping at various ports

cruiser Boat with at least a minimum of accommodations for overnight use

cruiser bollard Metal bollard with its two horns set off from one another at an angle

Cruising Permits Permits permitting entry and clearance into

Canada, issued by Customs authorities at first Canadian port entered

crutch Chock where spanker-boom rests

cuckolds neck Knot securing rope to spar, two parts of rope crossing and seized together; also called "cuckolds knot"

cuddy Small shelter cabin often found in the fore part of relatively open boats

cunning Directing the helmsman in the steering of a vessel (also spelled conning)

Cunningham Adjusts the tension of the leading edge of a sail causing it to change its shape; used to increase speed

current Horizontal movement of water

cutlass bearing A bearing used on a propeller shaft which allows water to flow around the shaft as a lubricant

cutter Small boat, similar to a sloop but with the mast further aft providing a larger area for headsails, normally sets two headsails, a forestay sail and a jib

cutting Tides are "cutting" when they are decreasing from spring tide to neap tide

cutwater Forward edge of the stem, particularly near the waterline

cyclone A storm or system of winds that rotates about a center of low atmospheric pressure

DELTA

D

D-S-T calculations Calculations involving distance, speed and time

dacron Trademark name for polyester

dagger Any timber that is diagonal in the frame

daggerboard Dagger-shaped board forced down vertically through its casing; used instead of a centerboard on small sailboats

dan buoy Flotation device on man-overboard pole

danforth Patented lightweight anchor

danger angle A plotting angle which indicates an unsafe condition

davits Arms with a "purchase" which can be swung out over the side in order to lift heavy objects

  cat davit Davit used to lift the anchor after it clears the water

Davy Jones locker The bottom of the sea

Davy Jones The spirit of the sea

daybeacon A large geometric marker on a piling to mark one side of a channel or an obstruction; also called "daymark"

daymark See "daybeacon"

daysailers Small sailboats without accommodations

day shapes Special markers hung aloft—black balls, baskets, cones and the like to indicate the vessel's type, occupation or state

day tug boat Used for short hauls, have no living accommodations

DC (abbr) Direct Current (electrical)

dead ahead A direction directly in front of the vessel

dead astern A direction directly in back of the vessel

dead calm Absence of any wind

dead door Door on the outside of a ship's quarter in order to keep out the sea should the quarter-galley be carried away

deadeye Circular piece of wood with holes to reeve lanyards of the rigging

dead flat Ship's widest cross-section; the midship frame

dead freight The amount paid for unoccupied space in a chartered vessel

dead head Using a rough piece of wood as an anchor buoy

deadlight 1. A fixed skylight 2. Glass used in a porthole when the porthole cannot be opened

dead men Old term for gasket-ends or reef-ends not being tucked in when furling the sail

dead neap Lowest point of a neap tide

dead on end Directly opposing the ship's course such as the wind is "dead on end"

dead reckoning To determine the vessel's position by using courses and distances from the last known position

deadrise The angle of the bottom of the boat from the keel outward as it rises compared to a horizontal line, expressed as the angle or inches per foot

deadrising Parts of the vessel's floor where the floor timbers terminate upon the lower futtock; also called "rising line"

dead sheave Scored aperture in the heel of a topmast through which a second top-tackle can be rove

dead-water Eddy under a vessel's counter when the vessel is in motion

dead weight That part of a heavier type of cargo which pays freight based on weight instead of bulk

deadweight tonnage Carrying capacity of a vessel determined by weight in tons of 2,240 pounds

dead wind A wind blowing from the point toward which a vessel is sailing

deadwood Blocks of timber, laid upon each end of the keel, where the vessel narrows

dead works The part of a ship above the water when fully loaded or in ballast; also called "upper works"

deck A platform on a vessel often serving as a structural element and forming a floor

flush deck *1. A deck that follows the sheer from the bow to the stern 2. Continuous floor from stem to stern upon which there are no structures*

deck beam A bridge between the sides which supports the deck

deck chair Folding chair often having an adjustable leg rest

deck eye Small eye attached to a plate which can be screwed onto the deck; also called "sash eye"

deck filler Flush fitting with a flush cap connected by pipe to tanks below deck; also called "pipe deck plates" and "filler"

deck hand Seaman who performs manual duties

deck head Underside of the deck which becomes the overhead of any compartments below

deck hook 1. Fastening hook secured to deck 2. The "compass-timber" bolted horizontally athwart a ship's bow, connecting the stem timbers and the deck planks of the fore part of the ship

deck house Superstructure on a ship's upper deck

decking Material used for a deck

deck light Thick glass fitted into the deck in order to provide light below

deck log Record of navigational information including various times, weather, wind, visibility, conditions, names of persons aboard

deck pipe Pipe through which the anchor line passes through the deck to the "chain locker"; also called "naval pipe"

deck shelf Planks on inside of vessel which support the ends of the deck beams; also called "clamps"

deck-stopper Secures the cable forward of the windlass while it is being overhauled

deck transom Transom which supports a deck

decommission To remove a vessel from service

deep 1. Any of the fathom points on a sounding line that is not a mark 2. A deep portion of any body of water. However, generally applies to long narrow ocean areas where the depth exceeds 3,000 fathoms

deep-sea Something occurring in deeper parts of the sea, such as deep-sea fishing

deep-sea-lead Used for deep soundings

deep-six Throw away, throw overboard

deep-vee hull Hull with multiple chines for a softer ride at high speeds

deep waisted When the quarterdeck and the forecastle are raised significantly above the level of the main deck

dee shackle A very common type of shackle, shaped similar to the letter "U", with a pin closing the open side

delaminated Separation of the fiberglass from a wooden core due to moisture penetration and possible rotting of the core

delta Used to indicate the letter "D"

Demarcation Lines Lines that have been established separating international and inland waters

departure You "take departure" from a known position to commence "dead reckoning"

depth A measurement inside the hull from the underside of the deck to the top of the keel, not the same as "draft"

depth(s) 1. Deep place in a body of water 2. Measurement from the surface to the bottom 3. The extent of the square sails from the headrope to the footrope

depth alarms An audible alarm signal on an electronic depth sounder activated whenever the water depth is less than the the the selected depth programed into the device

depth of water Distance from the surface to the bottom, not to be confused with "height of tide"

depth recorder A type of depth sounder which prints a permanent record of depths

depth sounder Electronic depth-finding instrument

derelict Vessel forsaken on the high seas

derrick Single spar used for hoisting

deviation Variance of compass needle from true north

devil's claw Claw type device which can be lowered onto chain immediately stopping its "pay out"; also called "chain hook"

dewatering device Electrical and mechanical bilge pumps plus manual devices such as cans, scoops, buckets

de-winterizing Re-commissioning a winterized boat by purging all systems of anti-freeze liquids

diagonal planking When one or more layers of wood forming the hull's skin is attached to the fore and aft planking adding substantial strength to the hull; see "cold moulding"

diamond knot Fancy bend made by interlacing the ends of two ropes

diesel engine Internal combustion engine in which air is compressed to a high temperature which then ignites the fuel injected into the cylinders

dinghy Small open boat often carried on a larger boat; also called "dink"

dink A contraction of "dinghy"; a small open boat carried on a larger boat

dirty wind The wind immediately to the lee of the sail or other object which is confused and non-directional; also called "wind shadow"

dismasted When a vessel's mast is carried away

displacement Vessels achieve buoyancy by displacing a volume of water equal to its weight

displacement tonnage Weight of water displaced by a vessel, the actual weight in tons of 2,240 pounds

distress signals Any type of signal indicating a vessel needs assistance

ditty bag Small bag for tools and personal items

ditty box Used for the same purpose as a "ditty bag"

dive boat A boat used primarily for divers, may have some specialized diving equipment aboard

diver Red flag with white stripe to indicate a diver is working in the area

dividers A small navigation device with two arms which can be separated and placed at two positions on a chart. Placing the open dividers on the chart's scale will indicate the distance between these two points

DMA (abbr) Defense Mapping Agency

dock The "water area" in which a boat lies when "made fast" to a shore installation

dockage Charge for the use of a dock

dock a vessel Making the vessel fast at a shore installation

docker A person connected with docks such as a longshoreman

dockhand One who works on docks

docking When a vessel is placed in a dock

docking plan A drawing showing where lifting slings and shoring blocks must be placed if the vessel is to be hauled out on a marine railway

dockland 1. The part of the port occupied by docks 2. A residential section adjacent to docks

dock lines Lines used to make a vessel fast to a shore structure; also called "mooring lines"

dockside Shore area adjacent to docks

dockworker A person who works on docks

dockyard A shipyard

documentation Federal registration for a vessel

dodger Canvas placed on the vessel to create a wind break for the crew

dog 1. A lever shaped or screw type locking device used on waterproof doors, hatches and portlights 2. Short iron bar with teeth at one end and ring at the other, used for a purchase

doghouse Raised portion aft in a trunk cabin which provides good visibility and can be used as a steering position

dog's body A kind of a boat with a square stern

dog shore Pieces of timber used to hold a ship in place before launching

dog vane Small vane normally used to show direction of the wind

dog watches Half watches of two hours each

doing an old man To bring the vessel on another tack by turning the ship's stern through the wind; also called "wear" and "wearing ship"

doldrums Parts of the ocean near the equator where light winds or dead calms prevail

dolphin A spar or buoy to which a vessel may bend its cable

dolphin striker Short, perpendicular spar, under the bowsprit end, used for guying the head-stays; also called the "martingale boom"

dorade box A box on which a cowl ventilator is mounted, air and water enters the box through the ventilator and is separated, only the air is allowed to enter the vessel

dory Flat-bottomed boat with high flaring sides, sharp bow and a deep "V" shaped transom

double To sail around something such as a cape so that the cape will be between the vessel and her previous position

double bank Two men working together in unison such as hauling on a line or rowing with the same oar

double banked Two oars, opposite the other, pulled by men seated on the same thwart

double bladed Canoe paddle with a "blade" at either end in order to more conveniently paddle on each side of a canoe

double block Pulley block with two sheaves on the same pin

double braid Rope made with a braided core and cover

double-decker Vessel having two decks above the waterline

double-ender Boat with stern and bow pointed, resembling one another

double Spanish burton Tackle having three double blocks

double tackle A purchase using two double sheave hook-blocks; also called "two-fold" purchase

double topsails Two sails on a square-rigged vessel corresponding in width to the topsail formally carried on a square-rigger but only half as high. The upper sail has a yard which may be hoisted or lowered but the yard of the lower sail is stationary

doubling A strip sewn into a sail in order to strengthen it

douse To lower suddenly

dousing chock Timbers joined together across the apron and lapped within the inside planking above the vessel's upper deck

down by the bow The vessel is too heavily loaded forward, same as "trims by the head"

down by the stern The vessel's stern draft is excessive; also called "trims by the stern"

downhaul Rope used to haul down jibs

downrigger Small fishing outrigger with a built-in reeling apparatus

downwind A direction to the leeward

dowsed When a sail is lowered quickly, same as "doused"

DR (abbr) Dead reckoning

draft Depth of water required for a vessel to float

draft marks Figures marked on the stem and the stern of vessel showing the depth of the vessel

drag A machine with a net used for dragging the bottom for lost items

dragger A fishing vessel which "drags" a trawl or a dragnet

dragnet A net towed along the bottom of the water by a "dragger", in order to catch fish

draw When a sail is filled by the wind

dredge Vessel designed to excavate the land under water

dress ship Hoisting a continuous line of flags from the bow to the stern of a vessel

drift 1. The velocity that a current flows 2. The amount of leeway a vessel makes 3. Being carried along by the current or wind

driftage Amount of deviation from a ship's course due to leeway

drift anchor Used to keep the bow into the wind, normally a canvas cone; also called a "drogue" and "sea anchor"

drift lead A lead line lowered with some slack while anchored, if line becomes taut, the anchor has probably been dragged

drift piece Upright pieces of timber which join the plank-sheer and the gunwale

drifts Pieces in the sheer-draught where the rails are cut off

drive To scud before a gale

driver Fore-and-aft spanker sail set at the stern of full-rigged ship

DRM (abbr) Direction of Relative Movement

drogue Open ended canvas cone used to slow the downwind drift of a boat in heavy weather and/or to keep the bow of the boat into the wind; also called a "sea anchor"

drop Depth of sail, head to foot, amidships

drop keel A retractable keel, centerboard, dagger board

drum A cylindrical and horizontal part of a windlass on which the line is wrapped; if vertical it may be called a "capstan"

drumhead The top of the capstan

dry A vessel which takes aboard little spray in heavy seas

drydock Dock area which can be pumped dry in order to make repairs to a vessel's bottom

dry rot Fungus which attacks "wet" wood

dub To reduce the end of a timber

duck Cloth for small sails, lighter and finer than canvas

dumb barge A work vessel which does not have any self-propulsion

dumb compass A "pelorus," which is a sighting device without a compass, used to determine relative bearing

dunnage Loose material, placed in a hold around stowed cargo in order to protect it

ECHO

E

E (abbr) East

earing A rope attached to the sail by which it is bent or reefed

ease Relieve or release from tension, weight, pressure or restraint; to make looser, move or shift slightly

ease a line To lessen the strain on a line and let it out slowly; also called "pays out" a line

ease a vessel Putting the helm hard alee or jettisoning some cargo or equipment in a heavy sea

ease away Slacken line gradually

ease her! Command to reduce speed

ease off Slacken line gradually

ease the helm Put the helm a little to amidships in order to relieve the rudder and the steering gear of some strain

ebb Tidal current flowing toward the sea; also called "ebb current"

Echo Used to indicate the letter "E"

echo sounder Electronically measures depth of water by emitting a sound from a transducer and determines the depth by measuring the time for it to return

eddy Circular motion in the water caused by the meeting of opposite currents

edged nailed The method of fastening the planks on a strip plank vessel

EHF (abbr) Extremely High Frequency (radio)

elbow Structural members connecting two parts that meet; also called "knee"

elbow in the hawse Twisting of two cables holding a vessel caused by her twice swinging the wrong way

electric stove Probably the safest for cooking but requires shore power or an auxiliary generating plant

electrolysis The destructive action on a vessel's metals as a result of the combination of different types of metal and salt water. This results in an electric current developing and running from one metal to the other

electronic charts A full nautical chart projected onto a viewing screen

electronic navigation Radar, loran and similar equipment used in navigation

engine alarm system A warning alarm indicating high temperature or oil pressure problems in the engine

engine bearer One of the sleepers supporting a large engine; also called "engine keelson"

engine beds Stout structural members running fore and aft on which inboard motors are mounted

engine compartment Compartment in which the engine is located; often will also house other equipment

engine keelson One of the sleepers supporting a large engine; also called "engine bearer"

engine logs Record of hours of operation, maintenance, troubles and repairs. Can assist in planning preventive maintenance

engine water pumps Circulate cooling water through the engine

ensign The flag flown which indicates the nationality of the vessel or its owner; also used to indicate the owner's membership in an organization such as a yacht club

entrance or entry Vessel's lines forward of the stem

EPIRB Distress beacon

epoxy A type of resin with excellent strength and adhesion

Equal interval light Navigation light with equal intervals of light and darkness; also called "Isophase"

equator A great circle of the earth equally distant from the two poles which divides the earth into the northern and southern hemispheres

> **cross the line** To cross the equator

equinox The time that the sun crosses the equator

estimated position A navigational point based on course, speed, drift

ETA (abbr) Estimated Time of Arrival

euvrou Wood used to extend the legs of the crow-foot to an awning

even keel When a vessel is so trimmed that she sits evenly in the water

external ballast Additional weight, normally lead, added onto the bottom of the keel

extra-tropical cyclone The principal source of foul weather in the U.S. It is a traveling system of winds rotating counterclockwise around a center of low barometric pressure and containing a warm front and a cold front

extruded mast A mast forced from the furnace in one piece

eye 1. Circular part of a stay or a shroud where it goes over the mast 2. A direction, as to sail in the "winds eye", to sail directly into the wind

eye and eye rigging screw Both ends of the rigging screw have "eyes"

eye and fork rigging screw One end of the rigging screw has an "eye" the other end a fork

eye bolt An iron bar with an eye on one end which is fastened to the deck or side, used to hook tackle (see "ring-bolt")

eyelet Can be just a hole placed in material but will normally have a grommet fastened in the hole

eyelet-hole A hole in the sail for the cringle or roband

eyelet punch Tool used to secure grommets in place

eyes of a vessel Extreme forward part of a vessel

eye splice A fixed loop spliced into the end of a line

FOXTROT
F

facing Letting one piece of timber into another with a rabbet

face pieces Pieces of wood on the fore part of the knee of the stem head. Closes any potential gap between the stem and the planking

fag or fagged When the end of a rope is untwisted; ragged ends of lines

fairing Checking the boat's lines to be sure they are clean and smooth after it is framed but before building it, any adjustments are made at this time

fairlead A block, ring or strip of plank with holes that serves as a guide for the "running rigging" or any of a vessel's rope; also called "fairleader"

fairway Navigable part of a river, bay or harbor

fairway buoy The outermost buoy which marks the beginning of a "fairway"

fair wind A wind that allows for easy sailing, not far aft or forward

fake Each loop of rope in a coil; also called "flake"

fake down To coil line down with the ends of the line overlapping so it will run freely without fouling; also called "flaked down"

fall That part of the tackle (rope) to which power is applied when using a "block and tackle"

fall aboard To strike the vessel's side

fall astern To move or be driven backwards

fall away To be driven sideways by the wind or current

fall calm To cease to blow, to become calm

fall down Sail toward the mouth of a river; to drift down a stream

fall home When the top-sides of a ship incline inward from the perpendicular

fall off The period during tacking when the vessel's head moves to the leeward and before it picks up speed again

false keel An extra timber fastened externally to the bottom of the keel in order to protect it; also called a "worm shoe"

false stem A piece fitted externally to the stem in order to produce a finer cutwater

false tack A trick in competitive racing when the crew goes through the motions of preparing to tack but remain on the same course

fancy-line Line rove through a block at jaws of gaff, used as a downhaul

fashion-pieces Aftermost timbers, forming the shape of the stern

fast A rope by which a vessel is secured

fastenings Screws, specially designed nails, bolts and similar items used to hold planks, equipment, cleats, chocks, and the like in place

fathom Six feet

fathometer Electronic instrument used to measure the depth of the water

faying Closely joining objects together

FBSA (abbr) Federal Boat Safety Act

FCC Rules Regulations governing radio equipment

feather A batten on the back of the mast to which the sail track is fastened

feather (feathering) an oar Turning an oar blade horizontally as it comes out of water

featheredged Planks which have one edge thicker than another

feathering propeller 1. Often used on sailboats to reduce drag, the blades of the propeller fold together when there is no engine propulsion being used 2. Variable pitch propeller sometimes used on motorboats

feather spray Spray cast up by the bow of a fast moving vessel

feed tank A secondary tank which holds the fuel just before going into the engine, often a gravity type tank above the engine

fellows Wooden pieces used between the spokes to make the rim of the steering wheel

fender boards Short lengths of planking hung over the side to provide a wider surface against a single piling,

fenders Relatively soft objects placed between the boat and another object in order to protect the vessel's topsides from damage; also called "bumpers"

fending off Pushing off, preventing the vessel from striking another object

ferro cement A method of hull construction using steel rods, wire mesh and a cement mix

ferry A vessel, often operating on a specific schedule and licensed by a governmental agency to carry passengers, vehicles and goods over a body of water

fetch 1. The distance traversed by waves without any obstruction 2. To hold a steady course on a body of water

fetch a compass Take a round about course

fetch away Shipboard articles breaking away and rolling to the leeward

fetch headway Making progress forward

fetch sternway Making progress backward

fiberglass Fiber reinforced plastic and resin

fid A tapered, pointed tool used in splicing

fiddle block A block with a long shell, with one sheave over the other, the lower one smaller than the upper one

fiddlehead Simple carved work (not figure-head), bending in like the head of a violin, at the prow of the vessel

fiddles Rails or battens used on a shelf to prevent items from falling off when a vessel heels

fife rail The rail around a mast

fighting chair Specially designed chair used in the aft cockpit of sport fishing boats to hold the fisherman in place when reeling in a large sport fish

figure-eight knot Usually in the end of a line, often used as a stopper to prevent the line from passing through a block

figurehead A carved figure over the cut-water

file scraper A scraper used to clean a vessel's bottom which has one end bent to allow pulling as well as a pushing movement

filler A flush fitting with a flush cap connected by a pipe to tanks below deck; also called a deck filler

fin keel A keel that looks like an inverted fish fin

fine lines A vessel with a narrow beam and a narrow entry

fine on the bows Anything bearing between dead ahead and 45 degrees towards the beam

fine reach Sailing when the wind is just forward of the beam

finger pier A narrow pier projecting from the shore

first mate Individual who is second in command, ranks after the Captain

first officer Same as "first mate," the officer after the captain

first watch 8:00 p. m. to midnight (2000 hours to 2400 hours)

fish 1. To raise the flukes of an anchor upon the gunwale 2. Strengthening a spar by fastening on other pieces

fish-block Tackle used for fishing an anchor; also called "fish-tackle"

fish-davit Spar or iron davit with a block and tackle at the end, used to fish an anchor

fisherman A large topsail used on schooners set above the main or mizzen

fisherman Vessel employed in the business of taking fish such as in the cod or whale fishery

fisherman's anchor Old type of anchor with a fixed shank, arms and stock

fisherman's bend A knot made by passing the end twice round a spar or through a ring and then back under both turns

fisherman's knot A simple but effective knot used to join two ropes

fish fall Tackle used on a fish davit

fish-hook A hook with a pennant, fish-tackle is hooked to the end of it (see fishing an anchor)

fishing an anchor Picking up an anchor by snagging it with another line

fishing banks Somewhat shallow areas in the sea such as the banks off of Newfoundland which are frequented by fishermen

fish-tackle Tackle used for fishing an anchor; also called "fish block"

fishwell A well, normally in the deck of the boat, in which caught fish or live bait can live, often will have a recirculating water pump to provide breathable water to the fish

fitting out Rigging and furnishing a vessel

fix Position of vessel, determined by bearings

fixed light A navigation light which does not flash

flag size Size of flag flown depends on the length of boat

at the dip *When flags are only partially hoisted up a signal mast*

flake Each loop of rope in a coil; also called "fake"

flake down To coil line down with ends overlapping so it will run freely without fouling; also "faked down"

flaking a mainsail Furling the sail by laying it in bights on both sides of the boom

flam The concave flare of the topsides just below the deck, increases deck size and reduces spray

flame arresters A screen-like device over the carburetor air intakes to prevent flame from coming into the engine compartment in the event of an engine backfire

flare 1. A pyrotechnic device which may show distress 2. The forward sides of a boat when they incline outwards to reduce the spray coming aboard

flashing lights A light buoy which is off for longer periods of time than being lighted, opposite of "occulting" light

flashing light signal Sending signals normally with Morse Code using long and short flashes of light for dots and dashes

flat A sheet is "hauled flat" when it is hauled down close

flat aback When a sail is blown with its after surface toward the stern

flat bottom One of the three basic bottom shapes—flat, round and vee

flats Large areas of shallow water

flat seam When two pieces of cloth are overlapped before being sewn

flattening agent Added to marine enamels if a less glossy finish is desired

flaw A gust of wind

fleet To come up on tackle and draw the blocks apart, for another pull, after they have been hauled to the two block position

Flemish eye A method in splicing an eye into the end of a rope

Flemish horse An additional foot rope at the ends of the top-sail yards

Flemish or Flemish down To coil a line spirally, laid flat on the deck resembling a mat

flinders bar Iron bar placed near a compass to reduce deviation caused by local influence

floating anchor A device that works as a drag which keeps the vessels bow into the wind; a "sea anchor"

floating dock 1. A dock which floats on the water but can be partially submerged in order to allow a vessel entry at which time it is again raised, a floating drydock 2. Type of dock often used in modern marinas which rise and fall with the tide along with the vessels attached to them

floating harbor Harbor enclosed by a floating breakwater

floating light A lightship

floating pier A pier which rises and falls with the tide

float plans Informing a friend of when and where you will be cruising, along with a good description of the vessel plus any changes when they occur

flogging A sail thrashing from side to side when the wind is directly ahead

flood anchor An anchor used during a flood tide

flood current The incoming tidal current is called the "flood"

flood mark High water mark

flood tide Rising tide as opposed to an ebb tide

floor Structural members in the bottom of boat, also "floor timbers," not used for walking upon as in a building, they tie together the keel and the lower ends of the frames

floorboards Planking laid upon the floors to provide a walking area, normally called the "sole"

floor head Outer end of the floor timbers

floor plan Drawing showing the water-line section of a vessel

floor timber A timber placed immediately across the keel

flotilla A fleet of small vessels

flotsam Wreckage debris floating on the water

flowing sheet When the vessel has wind "free" and the sheets are eased off

flowmeters Show fuel flow rate, good for determining most efficient speed and for keeping an accurate track of total fuel consumed

fluke Palm-shaped part of anchor at the end of the anchor arms

flush Level with

flush deck A deck that follows the sheer from the bow to the stern without any structures

flush hatch A hatch which is constructed to be set into and flush with the deck

flush ring Often used on deck hatches, the ring raises when lifted to pull upon the hatch but is flush with the hatch when not in use

flute Long vessel with flat ribs or floor timbers, round behind and swelled at the middle

fly 1. The horizontal length of a flag 2. "To let fly" as to let go suddenly and entirely

   let fly the sheets To let go the sheets suddenly and entirely

fly block A shifting pulley block

flying bridge An area above the level of the normal control center with an added set of controls and offering better visibility; also called "flybridge"

flying jib A sail outside the jib on an extension of the jibboom

flying jibboom An extension of the jibboom

FM (abbr) Frequency Modulation, radio

foam-core Used to stiffen flexible panels in fiberglass construction by separating two panels, thus producing a light, strong and stiff structure; also may use "balsa-core"

fodder To draw a sail, filled with oakum, under the vessel to stop a leak; also called "fother"

fog Vapor of fine particles of water suspended in the air near the surface of the water or ground. There are four types of fog—radiation, advection, coastal and steam

fog bank Mass of fog at sea, sometimes resembling land at a distance, which vanishes as it is approached

fogbound Unable to move a vessel due to fog

fogbow The indistinct circle of light sometimes seen in fog; also called "fogdog" and "fog eater"

fogdog Same as "fogbow"

fog eater Same as "fog bow"

fog horn 1. A horn kept aboard vessels to be used as a warning device to other boaters during foggy conditions 2. A permanently located horn sounded during fog conditions to warn vessels that are approaching the coast

following sea A sea which is running the same direction as the boat

foot The lower end of a mast or sail

footboards Wood placed across a boat's inside bottom for rowers to press feet against; also called "stretchers"

foothook Same a "futtock"

footrope Rope upon which to stand when reefing sail

foot-waling The inside planks over the floor-timbers

fore Located in the front of the vessel

fore and aft Lengthwise on a ship, from stem to stern

fore and after A ship with a "fore-and-aft rig," particularly a schooner

fore and aft rigged A vessel which does not use any square sails

fore and aft schooner A vessel "schooner rigged" with fore and aft sails

fore beam A short beam for supporting the deck in areas such as at a hatchway

forebody That part of the vessel forward of midships

forebrace Line to the fore yardarm for regulating the position of the foresail

fore cabin Cabin in fore part of a ship with accommodations being normally inferior to the aft cabins. On older vessels this would have been the crew's quarters

forecast Formalized weather prediction

forecastle The most forward cabin, the crew's quarters, pronounced "fo'-c's'l"

fore course 1. Another name for "foresail", the lowest sail on the foremast of a square rigged ship 2. The lower sail set abaft a schooner's foremast

foredeck Forward part of the main deck

forefoot The point where the stem joins the keel

fore-guy A guy may be called a "fore-guy" or an "after-guy" depending on its direction of pull

forehold A hold in the forward part of a vessel

foreland A cape or promontory jutting out into the sea

forelock Piece of iron driven through the end of a bolt to prevent its drawing

foremast The vessel's forward mast

forepeak Extreme forward compartment of a vessel

forereach 1. To go ahead of another ship when close-hauled 2. To gain ground in tacking

fore-runner A piece of rag, terminating the stray-line of log-line

foresail Another name for "fore course" 1. The lowest sail on the foremast of a square rigged ship 2. The lower sail set abaft a schooner's foremast

foresheet 1. One of the sheets of a foresail 2. The forward part of an open boat

foreship Fore part of a ship; the bow

foreshore The area on land that lays between low and high tides

forestays "Standing rigging" from the mast to the bow of a sailboat

forestaysail The sail attached to the forestay, similar to a jib

foretop Platform at the head of a ship's foremast

fore-topgallant The part next above the "fore-topmast"

foretopman Sailor on duty on the foremast and above

fore-topmast The mast next above the "foremast"

fore-topsail A sail above the "foresail"

foretriangle The triangular area bounded by the mast, deck and forestay

forewind A wind that drives a ship forward

foreyard Lowest yard on a foremast

forge To forge or shoot ahead

fork and fork rigging screw A rigging screw with a fork at each end which is connected between the chain plate and the shroud

fork beam Short beam for supporting the deck at areas such as hatchways

fork terminal A fitting on the end of a shroud line which attaches to a forked rigging screw

forward Direction to the bow

fother To draw a sail, filled with oakum, under a vessel in order to stop leak; also called "fodder"

foul Lines are "foul" when tangled, opposite of clear

foul-anchor When the cable has a turn around the anchor

foul another ship Getting in the way, impeding, entangling another vessel

foul ground A sea bottom which has debris, rocks, coral and the like which may easily foul an anchor

foul hawse When two cables are crossed, beyond the stem

foul water, to make Boating in water so shallow that the vessel stirs up the mud from the bottom making the water foul

founder The vessel fills with water from any cause and sinks

fox Made by twisting together two or more ropeyarns

Foxtrot Used to indicate the letter "F"

fractional rigging Forestay which does not attach to the top of the mast. Height of attachment is stated as a fraction of the distance up the mast from the deck (i.e. $7/8$th fractional rigging)

frames Wood set into the keel at a right angle which are then covered with planking; also called "ribs"

frap To pass ropes around a sail to keep it from blowing loose

free A vessel is "going free," when she has a fair wind, sailboat has the wind astern; also called "sailing downwind", "off the wind", "running"

freeboard Distance between the waterline and the top of deck

freeing port A hole in the bulwarks or toe rail which allows water to run overboard from the deck; also called "scupper"

freeing scuttle A scupper with a hinged cover on the outside which allows water to flow from the deck but keeps the sea water from entering

free wind To be able to sail free

French fake To coil rope with each fake (turn) outside the other

fresh breeze A wind blowing 19 to 24 mph

freshen Moving a rope to relieve it

freshen-ballast To shift ballast

freshen the hawse Apply new servings to the cable

freshen the way Increase speed

fresh gale A wind having a speed of 39 to 46 mph

fresh water cooled Engine contains its own fresh water and/or coolant in order to cool the engine. The heat is then transferred to the outside water by a "heat exchanger"

or "keel cooler"; also called "closed cooling"

frigate built A vessel with a quarterdeck and a raised forecastle

fronts Boundaries between air masses

fuel filter Removes dirt particles from the fuel before entering the engine

fuel pump Feeds fuel to the engine under pressure

fuel vapor detectors Provides a warning of dangerous fuel vapors which can accumulate in the bilge

fuel water separator Usually located on the suction side of the fuel system. Removes water from the fuel before entering the engine

full-and-by Sailing close-hauled on the wind

full-battened Sails in which the battens run from the leech to the luff

full bottomed Having a great capacity in the hull

full-length keel A keel running the full length of the vessel, normally on larger vessels and normally heavily ballasted

full rigged A vessel with three or more masts and carrying all square-sail except for the jib and spanker

full sailed All sails fully set

fume detector Warning alarm indicating explosive fumes are in the bilge

furl To roll a sail up snugly on a boom and secure it; also called "furling"

furling line Facilitates the turning of any furling stay

futtock The individual pieces used to form a "built" rib for a vessel

futtock hoop Band around a mast used for holding the futtock shrouds

futtock plank The plank next to the keelson on the inside of the frames, collectively all this inside planking is called the ceiling

futtock plates Iron plates crossing the sides of the top rim perpendicularly. The dead-eyes of the the topmast rigging are fastened to the the upper end and the futtock shrouds to the lower end

futtock shrouds Short shrouds coming from the lower part of the futtock-plates to the bend just below the top of the lower mast

futtock staff Wood or iron attached to the upper part of the rigging, to which the cat-harpin legs are secured

futtock timbers Timbers between the floor and naval timbers, and the top timbers

FWC (abbr) for a fresh water cooled engine; see "closed cooling"

GOLF
G

gaff 1. A spar holding the upper side of a four sided sail 2. A four-sided sail with its upper edge laced to a fore-and-aft spar 3. The spar upon which the head of a fore-and-aft sail is extended

gaff headed Any vessel with one or more gaff sails

gaff-rigged A four-sided sail with a spar holding the upper side; also called "settee rig"

gaff-topsail A light sail set over a gaff with its foot being spread by the gaff

gage 1. The depth of water of a vessel 2. The position of a vessel to another as having the weather or lee gage

gale A strong wind, rated depending upon its velocity, moderate (32 to 38 mph), fresh (39 to 46 mph), strong (47 to 54 knots) and whole (55 to 63 mph)

gallery Sort of a balcony projecting from the after part of the hull of a ship; called a stern or quarter gallery

galley Kitchen

galley built A flush deck sailing boat

galley pump Pump used to provide fresh or salt water to the galley; also called "pantry pump"

gallows-bitt Strong frame raised amidships to support spare spars; also called "gallows frame"

gallows-frame Same as "gallows-bitt"

gam Talking with someone who is on another ship

gammon, gammoning To fasten a bowsprit to the stem of a ship, as by iron bands or several turns of a rope

gammoning hole Hole in the knee of the head of the vessel through which the gammoning may be passed

gammoning plate An iron plate on the stem of the vessel to which the gammon shackles are fastened

gammon iron Clamp over the bowsprit securing it to the stem-head

gammon shackles Shackles for securing the gammon

gangboard Same as gangplank

gang casks Small casks used to bring water aboard

ganger Chain having one end attached to the anchor and the other end to the hawser

gangplank Temporary ramp between the vessel and a pier or wharf; also called "brow" and "gangway"

gangway On the vessel's side where people pass in and out of vessel, both the area and the walkway

gangway ladder Ladder down to the water from the vessel's gangway

gantline A rope rove through a single block, making a whip purchase; also called "girtline"

garboard plank Plank fastened next to the keel on the outside of a vessel's bottom

garboard strake The lowest strake (line of planking) next to the keel

garland Large rope lashed to a spar when hoisting it on board

garnet Purchase on the mainstay used for hoisting

gas vapor detector Detects dangerous gasoline fumes in the vessel's bilge

gaskets 1. Pieces of cloth or ropes used to secure a sail when it is furled 2. A packing material used to pack pistons or prevent fluid leakage

gather fresh away Vessel going on with increased velocity

gather way When a vessel begins to move through the water with increasing speed

gaub-line A rope leading from the martingale inboard; also called gob-line

gear A general term, meaning rigging

gel coat The outermost, thin layer of pigmented plastic which has a smooth and bright finish on a fiberglass boat

general charts Larger scale than "sailing charts" but still a rather small scale covering a large area, used for coastwise navigation outside of reefs and shoals but mostly within sight of land

generators, auxiliary Provide 120 volt electricity normally for cooking, heating and air conditioning; also called "genset"

genoa An overlapping jib

genset Another name for auxiliary generators

German eye splice A method of splicing an eye into the end of a rope

gib boom Same as jib-boom

gibe Change the position of the sails on a fore-and-aft vessel from one side to the other without going in stays; also spelled gybe or jibe

gib staff Staff to gauge the water or push a boat

gig Usually the officers' boat

gimbals Pivoted rings that allow the compass to remain relatively stable despite the boat's motion

gimblet To turn an anchor around by its stock

girt Moored by two cables to two anchors placed on opposite sides of the vessel to prevent the vessel from swinging

girth band Material sewn across a sail from the clew to the luff in order to strengthen it

girtline A rope rove through a single block aloft, making a whip purchase; also called "gantline"

give a wide berth Keep a safe distance from from some object or hazard

give way An order to men in a boat to pull with more force

gland A through-hull fitting for the drive shaft or rudder; also called a "stuffing box"

GMT (abbr) Greenwich Mean Time

go about Changing tacks when sailing close hauled

go to the bottom A wreck sinking out of sight

gob A sailor

gob-line A rope leading from the martingale inboard; also called "gaub-line"

goes by the board When something goes over the side

Golf Used to indicate the letter "G"

gong buoys Similar in construction to bell buoys, except they sound a gong

goose neck An iron ring fitted to the end of a yard or boom

goosewing Running with the wind, the mainsail and the headsail on opposite sides of the vessel

gore strake Any plank in the vessel's skin which tapers to a point before reaching the stem, considered poor construction

gores The angles at the end of goring-cloths (sail panels) that increase the breadth or depth of a sail

goring-cloths Pieces cut obliquely and put into the sail to add breadth to a sail, contemporarily called "sail panels"

GPS (abbr) Global Positioning System (a navigation system)

grab lines The lines around the outside of a lifeboat which allow people in the water to hold onto the boat

grab rails Fittings on cabin tops, sides and companionways onto which persons can hold while moving around the boat

grafting Covering a rope by weaving yarns together

grains Iron with four or more barbed points used for striking small fish

granny knot A faulty knot, often tied in error

grapnel anchor A small anchor with four or more flukes, used in dragging operations

grappling irons Crooked irons, used to seize and hold vessels fast

grating Open lattice work of wood, normally over hatches

graving Cleaning and painting a vessel's bottom

graving dock A dry dock

graving piece A new piece of wood inserted to repair damage

great circle An arc on the earth that is the shortest route

greave To clean a ship's bottom by burning

grinding Turning the handle of a winch

gripe Outside timber of the forefoot, under water, fastened to the lower stem-piece

gripes A vessel "gripes" when she tends to come up into the wind

griping spar A padded spar, used when a dinghy is suspended on davits, it is placed across the davits to prevent chafing of a dinghy's side

groins Embankments built out at an angle from the shore normally to prevent beach erosion

grommet A ring or eyelet

gross tonnage The total enclosed space of a vessel with each 100 cubic feet being a "ton"

grounds When a vessel touches bottom

ground swell A broad and deep undulation in the ocean often caused by a distant gale, become shorter and deeper in shoaling water

ground tackle Anchor, anchor rode and all gear used for attachment

ground timber Structural timbers attached to the keel of a vessel

ground ways The foundations in a shipbuilding yard on which the keel blocks are laid

Group flashing light Navigation light with two or more flashes separated by brief intervals and followed by a longer interval of darkness

Group occulting light Navigation light with intervals of light regularly broken by a series of two or more eclipses

grown spar A spar shaped from a single tree, thus not pieced

guard A strip of wood or other material added externally to the topsides in order to prevent damage from piers, pilings and the like; also called a "rub rail"

guard rails Any safety rails around the deck

gudgeon The fittings on the stern which support the rudder

guest flag Blue flag with a white stripe

gun tackle A purchase, two single blocks, giving power of two or three

gunnel See "gunwale"

gunwale Upper edge of side of boat, pronounced "gun'l"

goes by the board *When something goes over the side*

gusset A plate or bracket which holds two items together

guy Rigging line for control, attached to the end of a movable spar

gybe Change position of sails of a fore-and-aft vessel from one side to the other without going in stays; also spelled jibe or gibe

gyro compass A compass consisting of a continuously driven gyroscope whose axis is confined to the horizontal plane so that the earth's rotation causes it to assume a position parallel to the earth's axis and thus point to true north

HOTEL

H

hail 1. A call to another ship, a person "hails" another vessel to get its attention 2. "Hail from", the vessel is from a specific port, area or country

hailers An electronic megaphone used to communicate vocally between vessels or to shore; may be built-in or hand-held

hail from To come from some specific port, such as to "Hail from Somers Point, NJ"

hair bracket Molding extending aft from the figurehead

half board A maneuver of a sailing vessel to the windward by luffing up into the wind

half cowl ventilator Has the appearance of a cowl ventilator which has been cut in half, top to bottom, used on the deck against a cabin in order to cause less of an obstacle on the deck

half deck The deck immediately under the spar deck and next to the mainmast

half decked Partially decked over

half hitch Simplest knot, usually part of another knot

half mast A point below the top of the mast

half port One-half of a portlid for closing the portholes

halogen bulb Bulb filled with halogen gas which provides greater illumination

halon Contents of a fire extinguisher, which is an inert gas, used in engine compartments

halse To haul or raise

halser A hawser

halyard A line used to hoist a sail or spar aloft

hammock A piece of canvas a seaman sleeps upon

hand Person employed on a ship

hand a sail To furl a sail

hand-bearing compass A portable compass used for sighting

hand lead A weight, lowered into the water by hand to determine the depth of the water

hand-over-hand Hauling rapidly

handsomely Slowly and carefully in a proper manner

handspike Long wooden bar, used for heaving at the windlass

hand tight Moderately tight, as tight as can be made by hand

handy billy A watch-tackle

hanging knee A bracket placed under a deck to strengthen it

hanging locker A closet tall enough to hang full length garments

hanked on To rig or prepare a sail to be hoisted, the sail is "hanked on" or "bent-on", the boom or stay

hanks Rings around a stay

harbor An anchorage area affording some shelter from the wind and sea

harborage Shelter, harbor

harbor charts Largest scale chart showing a very limited area, showing rather detailed information on hazards and aids to navigation

harbor log That part of the log book covering the period during which a vessel is in port

harbor master Person in charge of anchorages and dock spaces including the general maintenance of the area

harbor reach The reach or stretch of a winding river which leads directly to a harbor

harbor watch An anchor watch

hard To do something fully and completely, such as "hard about"

hard alee An order to put the helm to the lee side; also called "luff alee"

harder the chine The more abrupt the angle is where the bottom and the topsides of the vessel meet at a well-defined area, the "harder the chine"

hard laid Rope which has been laid up tightly, not easy to splice

hard over All the way in one direction

hardtack Below average food

harping iron A harpoon

harpings Fore part of "wales" which encompasses the bows and fasten to the stem

harpoon A spear normally used on large fish

hatch or hatchway A deck opening providing access to space below

flush hatch A hatch which is constructed to be set into and flush with the deck

hatch bar Bar for securing a hatch cover

hatch beams Removable beams fitted across a cargo hatch which support the hatch covers

hatch boat Fishing boat with a well for holding the fish alive

haul 1. Alter the course of a vessel, to change the direction of sailing 2. Pull a boat ashore

hauled out Vessel is removed from the water

haul her wind When a vessel comes up close upon the wind

hauling 1. Pulling on a line 2. To haul the vessel from the water

hauling part The part of a fall on tackle to which power is applied

haul off Alter the vessel's course in order to get farther from an object

haul the wind Turn the vessel's head nearer the point from which the wind blows

having a bone in her teeth When excessive foam builds at the bow of the vessel which is underway (see bone)

hawse 1. That part of the ship's bow containing the hawseholes 2. Arrangement of anchors when the ship is anchored with anchors from each bow 3. The distance between the ship and the anchors by which she rides 4. The angle between the vessel's anchor line and its fore and aft line

athwart hawse When a ship lies across the stem of another, may be in contact or close

foul hawse When the cables cross each other or are twisted

freshen the hawse Apply new servings to the cable

hawse bag A bag of oakum used to plug the hawseholes in heavy seas

hawse-block Block of wood fitted into hawse-hole when at sea

hawse bolster A bolster or a block of iron or wood placed under a hawsehole to prevent chafing by the cable

hawse box The hawsehole (older term)

hawse buckler Iron plate or hinged shutter for closing the hawsehole

hawsehole Opening in the hull through which mooring lines are run

To come in through the hawseholes Beginning sea service at the lowest grade

hawse hook Breast-hook which crosses the hawse-timber above the upper deck

hawse-pieces Timbers through which the hawse-holes are cut

hawsepipes Fittings in the hawse-holes through which mooring lines are run

hawse plug A plug used for stopping the hawseholes, a "hawse block"

hawser Large diameter rope for dock lines on large vessels

cat hole Hole in the stern of a vessel for the play of the hawser

hawser bend The method of joining two heavy lines by seizings

hawser laid Rope laid, with nine strands, against the sun (same as cable-laid)

hawse timber An upright timber in the bow through which the hawse-hole is cut

hawse wood General term for the hawse-timbers

hawsing iron Caulking iron or chisel

hawsing mallet Mallet used in caulking

haze Punishing a man by keeping him unnecessarily at disagreeable work

head 1. Toilet and the toilet area 2. The bow 3. Upper ends of some of the vertical parts of the vessel

head and head Head on

head bay Space in a canal just above the lock

head boat A commercial fishing boat which takes individuals fishing for a fee with each individual paying their own fee. Usual trip is for 8 to 10 hours or less. Often called an "open boat". The opposite of a charter boat

head chute An older method of waste disposal using a canvas tube reaching from the head of the vessel to the water, through which refuse was carried overboard

headfast Line at the bow of a vessel to fasten it to a dock or other object

head foil Tubing which goes over the head stay which has grooves to hold the head sail, normally made of aluminum. More efficient and causes less wear on the sail and rigging than using "hanks" to secure the sail to the stay

head gate Upstream gate of a canal-lock

head gear Running gear of the sails set forward of the foremast

heading Direction in which vessel is pointed

head knee Pieces of molded knee-timber beneath the head rails for steadying the cutwater

headland A point of land projecting out into the sea; a cape

headledge Timber running athwart to frame hatchways

headliners Used in fiberglass boats to protect the overhead surfaces

head netting Ornamental netting sometimes used on the bow of a vessel

head rail One of the elliptical rails at the head of a ship

head reach To shoot ahead, as a vessel when brought to the wind and about to be put on another tack

headroom The distance from the deck to the "overhead"

headrope That part of the boltrope which terminates any sail on the upper edge to which it is sewn

headsail All sails forward of the most forward mast, such as a "jib"

head sea A sea coming towards the bow of a boat

head sheets 1. Any one of the sheets of the headsails 2. The flooring in the forepart of the vessel

headstay The foremost stay

head stick Short, round stick with a hole at each end, through which the headrope of some triangular sails are thrust before it is sewed on

head timber One of the upright pieces of timber inserted between the upper knee and the curved rail, to support the frame of the head rails

headway Forward motion of vessel

fetch headway Making progress forward

head wind Wind blowing in the opposite direction of the path of the vessel

head yard One of the yards of a vessel's foremast

heart Heart shaped block of wood used to reeve stays through

heart-yarns The center yarns of a strand

heat exchanger Method of exchanging heat from one system to another (i.e. using heated engine coolant to heat water in the fresh water system)

heave Throw or pull

heave taut Turn the capstan until the cable becomes strained

heave a cable short Hauling in so much cable that the vessel is almost over its anchor

heave a ship ahead Bringing the ship ahead while not under sail by using hawsers, cable and anchors

heave a ship astern Bringing the ship backwards while not under sail by using hawsers, cables and anchors

heave a ship down Careening a vessel by using tackle from the masthead to the shore in order to clean or repair her bottom

heave a strain To heave taut

heave about To put the vessel on another tack

heave away! Order to commence or continue heaving

heave ho! Cry of sailors when hoisting the anchor

heave in sight To appear or to come within sight, such as a ship at sea

heave out! Order for sailors to get out of their bunks

heave the lead Sounding with a lead line

heave the log Throwing the towing device overboard for a "chip" or "patent log"

heave in Pull in all the slack in a line and "take a strain" on it

heave in at the capstan To go around with it by pushing with the breast against the bars (poles that used to be used to turn large capstans)

heave-in stays To go about, tacking

heaver Short wooden bar, tapered at each end, used as a purchase

heave short To heave in on the cable until the vessel is nearly over her anchor

heaves to, heaving to Reducing headway and lying with the bow slightly off from directly meeting the oncoming waves; setting the sails to make little headway

heaving lines Light lines used for throwing between vessels or the shore, usually weighted at one end

heavy sea When the surface of a body of water is broken into a number of large waves

heavy weather Stormy, windy

heel chain Chain that connects the heal of the jibboom with the bowsprit

heel or heeling A sideward inclination normally of a temporary duration, common when sailing

heeling error Changing deviation in a compass due to heeling

heelpost Post supporting the outer end of a propeller shaft

height of tide Vertical measurement between the surface and the "tidal datum", normally MLLW (mean lower low water)

height of wave Measured from the trough to the crest

helm The steering mechanism of the vessel

at the helm *When someone is at the controls of the vessel*

ease the helm *Put the helm a little to amidships in order to relieve the rudder and the steering gear of some strain*

helm amidships *Order to keep the rudder fore and aft of the vessel*

port the helm *Order to put the helm toward the port (left) side of the vessel*

put the helm down *To push the helm down to the lee side in order to bring the vessel about or to bring her into the wind*

right the helm *Center the steering wheel*

shift the helm *Order to put the helm from one side to the other*

starboard the helm *Order to put the helm toward the starboard (right) side of the vessel*

up with the helm *Order to put the helm aweather*

helmless Without steering

helm's alee An order to let the head-sails fly in the wind in preparation of bringing the vessel about

helm-port Hole in the counter through which the rudder head passes

helmsman Individual at the controls of the vessel

helmsmanship Ability to steer well

hemp Cordage made from the fiber of a hemp plant

high Area of high atmospheric pressure

high and dry When a vessel is grounded above the water mark

high hat sections Used as stiffeners in fiberglass construction

high seas Open part of an ocean or sea outside of territorial waters

high tide Highest level of water reached

high water High tide

HIN (abbr) Hull Identification Number

hitch Knot attaching line to cleat, ring, spar

hobby horsing A vessel which is rocking violently fore and aft while going into a head sea

hog Flat, rough broom for scrubbing the bottom of vessels

hogged Said of a vessel, strained and drooping at each end; also called "arched"

hog pins Metal clips used around a bungee cord in order to create a loop

hoist The inner vertical side and the vertical dimension of a flag

hold, holds Compartments below deck, normally on larger vessels, used solely for carrying cargo

hold tack To continue on the present course or tack

holding tank Storage tank for sewage

hold-water Stop progress of boat by keeping the oar-blades in the water

holystone Large stone used to clean wooden decks

home 1. Sheets of sail are "home" when clews are hauled chock out to the sheave-holes 2. An anchor comes home when it is hove in

homing Steering a course by using a direction finder

hood 1. Covering for companion hatch and skylight 2. Foremost and aftermost planks of a ship's bottom, both inside and outside

hood-ends Ends of planks which fit into rabbets of the stem; same as "hooding-ends"

hook Slang for anchor

hook and butt Laying ends of timbers over each other

horizontal angle An angle between two landmarks, providing a line of position

horizontal load The horizontal load a vessel puts on the anchoring system

horn buoys Buoys using an electrically operated horn

horns The jaws, booms, gaffs, end of crosstrees

horn timber A timber which joins the sternpost to the transom

horse latitudes Calm areas between the trade winds and the westerlies in the higher latitudes

horseshoe buoy Life buoy shaped like a "U"

Hotel Used to indicate the letter "H"

hounds Projections at the masthead, shoulders for trestle-trees to rest upon

hour meter A meter which indicates the hours that an engine has operated

house a mast To lower it half its length, lashing it to the mast below

houseboats A boat which offers more living space than normal, often at the sacrifice of seaworthiness

house-line A small rope of three yarns used for seizings; also called "housing"

housing A small rope of three yarns used for seizings; also called "house-line"

hove in stays When a vessel is going from one tack to another; also called "in stays"

Hovercraft A vessel which "floats" on an air cushion above the sea caused by the downward pressure from the craft's propellers

how the wind blows or lies The direction or velocity of the wind

HP (abbr) Horsepower

hull The body of a vessel

> *take up* When the hull's planks swell from being placed in water, the seams "take up" and become watertight

hull down When upper section of a distant vessel is visible but the hull is not, due to the curvature of the earth

hurricane High intensity, revolving, tropical storm in the Atlantic Ocean with minimum winds of 74 mph

hydraulic steering Provides a force in a steering system using hydraulics to assist in turning the vessel

hydrofoil High speed boat that raises out of the water and rides on submerged foils which greatly reduces the drag of the water

hydrographic chart A marine chart used by navigators

hydrography Science of surveying the waters of the earth

hydrophobia The fear of water

hydroplane Powerboat designed for racing which has special planing surfaces to reduce "drag"

hypothermia Subnormal temperature within the central human body, caused by immersion in cold water

INDIA

I

I/O (abbr) Inboard type motor mounted in the hull with an external driving unit similar to the lower section of an outboard engine; also called "stern-drive," "outdrive," "inboard-outboard"

ice buoys Buoys used in the winter in areas of severe icing, very sturdy construction, may be lighted or unlighted

ICW (abbr) Intracoastal waterway

illustrated log Adding photos and/or drawings to the "deck log" for added interest

impeller 1. Gives a signal for the speed to a transducer 2. A principal part of a pump which moves liquid

in ballast When a vessel is not carrying cargo and adds ballast to lower the center of gravity, formally used rock, modern ships use sea water in tanks

inboard 1. More toward the center of a vessel 2. The engine is mounted within the hull of the vessel

inboard cruiser A cruiser with inboard motor propulsion

inboard-outboard The motor is an inboard type motor mounted in the hull, the driving unit is external and similar to the lower section of an outboard engine; also called I/O, outdrive, stern-drive

in chains Refers to an individual using the lead line and standing in the chain locker

incinerators Burn and reduce to ash the liquid waste pumped into them from marine toilets

inclinometer A pointed pendulum on an arched, graduated scale which indicates the angle of any heel

India Used to indicate the letter "I"

inhaul Any line use to bring a sail or spar inboard

in irons Sailboat that loses headway and stalls while coming about due to the wind being directly ahead

inland rules Rules of the road in harbors, lakes, inland waterways

inlet 1. A bay or recess in the shore 2. Narrow passageway between peninsulas or barrier islands allowing entry to an enclosed area such as a bay

innavigable Unnavigable; impassable for vessels

in shore Close to the shore

in stays A sailing vessel while going from one tack to another while her head is into the wind; also called "hove in stays"

interfaced Method by which navigation equipment can communicate with one another

intermediate shrouds Shrouds attached to the mast just below the upper spreaders if there are two spreaders

internal halyard A halyard inside of the mast instead of the conventional manner which is on the outside

international code A system of signals between vessels using flags and Morse code

in the teeth of the wind Same as to "sail in the wind's eye"

in the wind's eye To sail directly into the wind, same as "in the teeth of the wind"

Intracoastal waterways Bays, rivers, canals along the coast that are connected

inverter Changes DC to AC electrical current

IOR (abbr) International Offshore Rules, a set of rules for a class of racing

Irish pendant Any loose and tattered end of flags, pendants, ropes flying in the breeze

ironbound A dangerous coastline which does not offer landing areas to small boats

iron sick A vessel with its bolts or nails so corroded with rust that it has become leaky

isobars On a weather map, lines drawn connecting places of equal atmospheric pressure

isogonic lines Lines on chart, connecting points of equal magnetic variation

Isophase light Navigation light with equal intervals of light and darkness; also called "equal interval"

JULIETT

J

jack 1. Common term for the jack-cross-trees 2. A sailor 3. Small flag containing the union of a national flag displayed on the jack staff

jackass A hawse-bag

jackass rig Any unusual combination of masts or sails

jack block Block used in sending topgallant masts up and down

jack-cross-trees Cross-trees at the head of the long topgallant masts

jackrope A lacing that bends the foot of mainsail to the boom

jack-screw A purchase, used for stowing cotton

jackstaff At the bowsprit, upon which Union Jack is hoisted

jack stands Individual, adjustable stands used to support vessels when stored on land

jackstays Taut ropes along a yard to bend the head of the sail

jack tar Nickname for a sailor with little knowledge of seamanship

jackyard A spar extended above the gaff used to provide greater spread to a topsail

jackyard topsail An oversized gaff topsail using "clubs" to extend the mast and the gaff; also called "club topsail"

Jacobs ladder A rope ladder over the side

jamb cleat A cleat which jambs a line in a taper

jaw rope Ropes around the mast and through eyelets on the gaff sail which hold the sail to the mast; also called "parrel"

jaws Inner ends of booms, hollowed to go around the mast

jet engine A boat engine that acts as a pump which circulates sea water through it at a high rate of speed thus achieving propulsion

jetsam Items and equipment deliberately thrown overboard

jettison Throw overboard

jetty Structure or embankments projecting out from shore to protect a harbor entrance

jetty-head The projecting part of a jetty or wharf

jewel blocks Single blocks at the yard-arms, used with studdingsail halyards

jib A single "headsail", a triangular sail, set on the headstay

jibboom A spar that forms an extension of the "bowsprit", tack of the jib is lashed to it

jib downhaul A block and tackle arrangement used to lower the jib

jibe Change position of sails of a fore-and-aft vessel from one side to the other without going "in stays"; also called gybe or gibe. If done accidently it can be dangerous

jib furling gear Consists of a swivel at the top and a rope operated reel at the bottom of the jib stay, pulling the rope on the reel will furl or unfurl the jib

jib-headed Any sail plan with a forward jib, such as a sloop or ketch

jib iron An iron hoop which moves along the bowsprit to which a flying jib is attached

jib of jibs The outermost jib being used when there are three or more in use

jib outhaul A line on the jib boom which hauls out the jib iron to which the jib is attached

jib stay A forestay to which the jib is attached

jib topsail Small jib set between the mast and the boom which flies from the end of the flying-jib boom

jiffy reefing A quick method of reefing the mainsail by using lines that are permanently attached to the sail

jigger 1. Small square sail on a mast 2. A boom at the stern of a vessel

jigger mast 1. Aftermost mast of a four-masted ship 2. Small stern mast of a yawl

jolly boat Small boat normally on coasting vessels, hoisted at the stern

jon boat Row boat that generally has a square bow and stern, approximately 12 feet long

Juliett Used to indicate the letter "J"

jumper stay Supports the top of the mast above a fractional rig. Works off of jumpers which are like little spreaders

jury mast A temporary replacement for a mast that has been carried away. Often made by splicing two sections of a broken mast together

jury mast knot Often used to take the stays and shrouds of a temporarily rigged mast; also called a "shamrock knot"

jury rig Temporary rigging used with a "jury mast"

jury rudder A method which temporarily replaces the vessel's normal steering system when the rudder is inoperable

KILO

K

keckling Old rope wound around cables to prevent chafing

kedge 1. A type of anchor 2. Moving boat by hauling on the anchor rode 3. Any type of anchor carried out from a grounded vessel to be used in "kedging"

kedging Moving a boat by hauling on the anchor rode. An anchor is carried out from a grounded vessel and the anchor line is pulled upon to assist in refloating the boat

keel The main longitudinal member of the hull; the body of the vessel

fin keel *A keel that looks like an inverted fish fin*

full length keel *Runs the length of the bottom of the vessel*

shield keel *Short keel with a bulge at the bottom for added stability*

shoal keel *Short, stubby keel, good for shallow water*

wing keel *Keel is more shallow than normal with a lead wing at the base for stability*

keel boat Boat decked over and having a keel. Used to transport freight on rivers and canals

keel cooler Removes the heat for the engine's internal cooling system and transfers it to the outside water; works similar to a "heat exchanger"

keel doubler A plank slightly wider than and attached to the inside of the keel, forms a ledge for the garboard strakes

keelhaul To haul a man or woman under the bottom of the vessel (not normally practiced any longer)

keel piece One of the pieces composing the keel

keelrake Same as keelhaul

keelson Timber placed on top of the keel and running parallel with it in order to strengthen the keel; also called an "apron"

cross keelson *Strong timber laid across the keelson to give support to heavy equipment and engines*

keelson topping *Timber laid on top of the keelson for added strength*

kellet A weight sent half-way down the anchor rode in order to lower the anchor's angle of pull; also known as a "sentinel"

ketch A two-masted sailing rig with a shorter after mast

kevel Piece of wood, bolted to a timber, used for belaying ropes; also called "cavil"

kevel heads Timber-heads used as kevels

killick A general name given to anchors

Kilo Used to indicate the letter "K"

king of knots The bowline

king plank Center plank on a laid deck

king spoke Topmost spoke of steering wheel with the rudder centered

kink A twist in a rope

KM (abbr) Kilometer

knees Structural members connecting two parts that meet, such as the sternpost to the keel; also called "elbow"

knight heads Timbers next to and on each side of the stem, forms support for the bowsprit

knittles Small rope used for seizings and hammock clews; also called "nettles"

knot 1. A unit of speed 2. Bends, splices and hitches

fisherman's knot A simple but effective knot used to join two ropes

king of knots The bowline

LIMA

L

labor When a vessel rolls or pitches heavily and makes little headway

lacing Rope used to lash a sail to a spar

laden in bulk Cargo is stowed loose in the hold

lading Loading, cargo or freight

laid down The lines of a vessel are "laid down" before she is built

laid up When a vessel is decommissioned for a period of time

land To go on shore from a vessel; to disembark

land breeze A current of air coming from the shore toward the sea

landfall Reaching the coast

land ho! Cry when land is first sighted

landing and lands The overlap of the planks on a clinker built boat

landing charges The charges and/or fees for landing of goods

landing craft Any of many vessels designed, often for military use but having commercial applications, to land men and equipment on the shore

landing place A place for landing people or goods from a vessel

landing stage A floating platform attached to a wharf, adjusting to the tide, for the landing of passengers or goods from a vessel

landing strake The second plank below the gunwale

landlubber A person with little knowledge of the sea

landmark A fixed object ashore which can be used as a reference point

lands and landing The overlap of the planks on a clinker built boat

land shark A swindler who makes seamen his primary victims

landsman or landman 1. One who lives ashore and knows little about the sea 2. An inexperienced sailor

landward Toward the land or on the side towards the land

land wind A wind coming from the land

lang's lay Wire rope in which the the wires in the stands and the strands are both laid right handed. This results in more wire being exposed, thus longer lasting rope

lanyards Ropes rove through deadeyes for setting up rigging

lapstrake Overlapping the planking on a vessel's side; also called "clinker built"

larboard The left side of a vessel, the port side. Old name still used by some but has been changed to "port" side so as to not be confused with "starboard"

latchings Loops on the head rope of a bonnet by which it is laced to the foot of the sail

lateral resistance The resistance by a hull from being driven sideways

lateral system of buoyage The system normally used in the U.S.A. The buoys indicate the direction to a danger relative to the course which should be followed, see "cardinal" system

latitude Distance north or south of the equator

launch To put a boat into the water

launching-ways Timbers placed beneath the vessel when building or launching it; also called "bilgeways"

lay 1. To come or to go, lay aloft 2. The twist of a stranded rope

lay a course A sailboat "lays her course" when she can reach her destination without tacking

lay aft Go to the stern of the vessel

lay day A day allowed to a person chartering a vessel in which to load or unload cargo or belongings

lay off To turn the vessel from any point

lay on oars Stop rowing

lay the land When the land seems lower due to sailing away from it

lay to Stop the motion of a vessel and cause her to become stationary

lazarette Small storage compartment at the stern, a locker under the cockpit seats

lazy jacks System of lines and pulleys that keeps the lowered mainsail on top of the boom

lead A shaped weight on a marked line used to measure depth

cast the lead Taking a sounding of the depth of the water with a lead line

heave the lead Sounding with a lead line

leading beacons Two beacons which when kept lined up with each other will lead the vessel to a safe passage

leading cleat A cleat which is open at the top in order to lead the line through the cleat before making the lines fast to the cleat's "horns"

leading wind Applied to a fair wind abeam or quartering

lead mine An unstable, narrow, deep draft vessel that requires considerable ballast for stability, not used as a complement

league Unit of length equivalent to three nautical miles

leather Leather or rubber placed around the loom of an oar where it rests in the oarlock to reduce wear on the oar

ledges Small pieces of timber placed athwart-ships under the decks, between the beams

lee 1. Protecting shelter 2. The side that is sheltered from the wind

bring by the lee To incline so rapidly to the leeward of the course as to bring the lee side suddenly to the windward and by laying the sails aback, exposes the vessel to capsizing

by the lee Drifting so as to let the wind strike the wrong side of the sails

under the lee On that side sheltered from the wind

lee beam The direction to the leeward, at right angles to the keel

leeboards Like external centerboards, one on each side, only lower one at a time—the "lee" board

leech 1. The after edge of a fore and aft sail 2. Either vertical edge of a square sail

leech line Rope used for hauling up the leech of a sail

leech rope That part of the boltrope which has the leech of the sail attached

lee helm Tendency of sailboat to turn the bow to leeward

lee helmsman When the helmsman sits downwind of the wheel or tiller

lee lurch When the wind and the waves throws the vessel to the leeward

lee-o An order: "We are going about"

lee shore Shore upon which the wind is blowing

lee side The side of the vessel away from which the wind is blowing

lee tide The tidal flow and the wind are in the same direction

leeward Toward the lee, the direction away from which the wind is blowing

leeway Sideways drift of boat caused by the wind or current

left-hand lay Stranded rope with the twist to the left, opposite the norm

lend-a-hand Assist

length of wave The distance between crests

length on the waterline Vessel length measured along the waterline; also called "load waterline"

let fly An order to immediately free the sheets in order to have the sails instantly spill their wind

let go by the run To loosen and let fall freely, such as a sail

liberty Leave to go ashore

lie at anchor Same as "at anchor"; a vessel when she rides by her anchor or is anchored

lie-to To stop the progress of a vessel at sea by counteraction of sails and helm; also called "lying to"

life boat Boats fitted to davits, used solely for emergencies

lifebuoy A ring or horseshoe-shaped, flotation device, often thrown to persons who have fallen overboard

lifelines Used at the edges of the deck to prevent people from falling

overboard, normally made from plastic covered wire rope supported above the deck by stanchions

life preservers A flotation device which provides buoyancy to keep a person in the water afloat

liferails Same purpose as "lifelines" except they are made of a solid material such as wood or metal

lift When the wind strikes sails on their leeches and raises them slightly

lifting eye cleat A typical cleat with "horns" on which lines can be fastened but it has a circular "eye" between the "horns"

lifting eyes Eye bolts on smaller boats which can be used to lift the boat out of the water. Should normally only be used with a davit

lifts Lines from the yard-arms to the mast-head used to support and move the yard

lighter Craft used for loading and unloading vessels; often a large flat bottomed barge

lighterage 1. Removing or loading cargo by lighter 2. Cost of transporting by lighter 3. Vessels engaged in lightering

lighterman A manager or an employee who works on a lighter

lighthouse A structure, often a tower, which shines a bright light as a warning or as a guide to mariners

light keeper One who cares for the light at a lighthouse or on a lightship

lightman A light keeper

lights Lighthouses or beacons

lightship Ship equipped with a brilliant light and moored in an area dangerous to navigation

  floating light *A lightship*

Lima Used to indicate the letter "L"

limber board A plank covering used to keep a vessel's limber from becoming filled with dirt

limber chain or clearer A chain run through the "limber holes" on a larger vessel which keeps the "limber holes" clean when it is pulled back and forth

limberholes or limbers Drainage holes in the bilge timbers, allows water to run to low point

limber strake The breadth of planking nearest to the keelson in a ship's hull

line Rope, the term "rope" is used very little aboard a vessel

  ease a line *To lessen the strain on a line and let it out slowly, also "pays out" a line*

  ease away *Slacken line gradually*

  ease off *Slacken line gradually*

  render a line *To ensure that a line will pass freely through a hole or a block*

  take a strain *When all the slack in a line is pulled in and an individual begins to exert pressure on the line*

line counter A device with gears that measures line when it is being purchased

line markers Markers inserted under a strand or two in the anchor line at fixed intervals which indicates the amount of line paid out

liquid petroleum gas (LPG) Excellent for cooking but can be dangerous if not installed and operated properly

list A vessel's continuous leaning to one side

livewell A well, normally in the deck of the boat, in which live bait can live. Often will have a recirculating water pump to provide breathable water to the fish; also called "baitwell"

lizard A length of line with a round thimble at one end through which a line can be rove

LOA (abbr) length over all, maximum length of vessel's hull

load line Markings on the side of a ship indicating the safe limit of cargo which may be loaded; also called "Plimsoll line"

load waterline Vessel's length measured along the waterline; also called "length on the waterline"

lock An enclosure with walled sides and gates in which the water level may be raised or lowered in order to allow vessels to pass in otherwise non-navigable waters

lockage 1. Toll for using a canal's lock 2. Amount of elevation and descent made by the locks of a canal 3. Process of passing vessels through locks 4. A system of locks

lock bay Water held by a lock

lock chamber Area inside of the walls and gates of a lock

locker A storage place; closet; may also include chests and boxes

locker ring A ring fitted into a metal plate to make a simple opening handle for lockers and hatches

lock gate A gate used to open or close a canal or river lock

lock hatch Perpendicular sliding board in the sluice-gate of a canal lock

lock paddle A small sluice used to fill and empty a lock

loft A large flat area used for making and repairing sails

log A device used for measuring distance and speed

  chip log *Older method of determining a vessel's speed by towing a specially designed board from the stern. Speed is determined by the* amount of log line run out during a fixed period of time

heave the log Throwing the towing device overboard for a "chip" or "patent log"

taffrail log A speed log attached to the taffrail of the vessel

log book Journal kept by the chief officer

loggerhead Timberhead in a whaleboat around which the harpoon line is taken

log line The line from the stern to a "chip log" or "patent log"

long-board A long tack

longboat Another name given to a ship's launch; the largest boat on a merchant vessel

longitude The distance east or west of the Meridian of Greenwich

long line A single fishing line with perhaps hundreds of fish hooks from the top down to its bottom

long shackle Made the same as other shackles except that it is longer than normal

long shaft An outboard motor when the shaft is longer than normal, often used on sailboats where the normal length shaft would not extend into the water

longshore (short for alongshore) 1. Employed along the shore, such as a longshoreman 2. Living along a coast

long splice Joins two lines in such a way that the final splice is no thicker than the original line

long top-timber The timber above each of the first futtocks

loof That part of boat where the planks begin to bend as they approach the stern

loom 1. That part of oar within the row-lock 2. The exaggerated appearance of something on the horizon or through darkness and fog

loose footed When the lower end of a sail is not attached to a boom

loose sail When the sail is unfurled

LOP (abbr) Line of position

Lop A small, fast, sloppy sea

loran Long range navigation system

low water Low tide

lower boom Outward rigged spar to which small boats may be fastened; also called "boat boom"

lower futtock timbers Timbers between the floor and the top timbers

lower half cants Those parts of the frames forward and abaft the floor timbers which cross the keel

lower mast The main mast when more than one section is spliced together

lower shrouds Shrouds attached to the mast just below the spreader or the lower spreader if there are two spreaders

lower the yards a portoise Lower the yards to the gunwale

LPG (abbr) Liquified petroleum gas

lubber A greenhorn aboard a ship

lubberly Doing something in an ignorant or sloppy manner

lubbers line The fore-and-aft line of a compass

luff The forward leech of fore-and-aft sails

luff alee An order to put the helm to the lee side; also called "hard alee"

luff and touch-her To bring a vessel up and see how near she will go to the wind

luffing When the forward edges of sails shiver or shake due to the vessel being pointed too close into the wind

luff tackle Composed of a double and single block

luff up 1. Point the forward edge (luff) of a fore-and-aft sail into the wind 2. Point the bow into the wind

luff-upon-luff A luff-tackle applied to the fall of another

lugger A small fishing or coasting vessel that carries one or more lugsails

lugger tug boat Tug boat designed for towing with a hawser

lugsail Four sided sail bent to a obliquely hanging yard that is hoisted and lowered with the sail attached

lunch hook Informal name for a light anchor used during temporary stops

lurch Sudden rolling of a vessel to one side

LWL (abbr) Length on the waterline; also called "load waterline"

lying to To stop the progress of a vessel at sea by counteraction of sails and helm; also called "lie to"

 MIKE **M**

M (abbr) Meter

macerator-chlorinator Grinds up the waste from marine toilets and treats it with a disinfectant

made fast Tied up

made mast Refers to a solid wood mast in which more than one piece of timber is spliced together; also called "built mast"

magic box A purchase contained within a box with fixed pulleys, used to make minor sail adjustments

magnetic bearing The compass bearing of an object

magnetic compass A compass with a magnetic needle which points toward magnetic north, subject to some variation and deviation

magnetic course A course using magnetic north as its base

magnetic meridian A line of force along which the needle of a compass settles

Magnetic North The direction a compass would point if it was not subject to any local interference

magnus hitch A clove hitch with an extra turn

main The principal mast and sail

main beam Beam forward of the main hatch, being the transverse measure of the vessel

main boom The mainsail's boom

main brace Brace sustaining the mainyard

main course Another name for the mainsail

main deck The upper deck

main frame The largest rib which is also the first one set by the builder, the largest section of the frame

main halyard Halyard used to raise the mainsail

mainland The continent, the principal land as opposed to an island

mainmast A sailing vessel's principal mast

mainsail The principal sail on the boat

mainsheet The line used to control the mainsail towards the aft part of the boom

mainsheet traveler A track to which the lower block of the mainsheet is attached in which it may be moved back and forth while tacking

mainstay A ship's stay extending from the maintop forward to the foot of the foremast

maintop Top of the mainmast sometimes with a platform for the convenience of men aloft

mainyard The yard supported by the mainmast on which the mainsail is extended

make and mend A half day off given to seamen for them to mend their clothing

make foul water Boating in water so shallow that the vessel stirs up the mud from the bottom making the water foul

make haste Bear a hand

make land To discover land as a vessel approaches it from the sea

make rooming Same as "rooming," increasing the distance off the lee shore to ensure that the wind does not jeopardize the safety of a vessel

make sail Sails are hoisted

make water Vessel is leaking

making Said of a rising tide

making colors Ceremonial raising of the flag at 8:00 a.m.

making iron Caulking iron used to harden oakum

making leeway Slipping sideways

mallet Small maul, made of wood, may be used in caulking

manilla A natural fiber from the Philippines used extensively in the making of rope; has been replaced to a great extent on pleasure craft in recent years by synthetic lines

man in the chains Refers to the individual using the lead line and standing in the chain locker

manrope knot A fancy knot that can be used as a handhold on a "manrope"

manropes Ropes used in going up and down a vessel's side

manufacturer's certification of compliance Only boats and equipment subject to federal standards are required or allowed to display. Includes manufacturer's name and address, and "This (boat or equipment) complies with the U. S. Coast Guard safety standards in effect on the date of certification"

MARB Marine Assistance Request Broadcast is broadcast by the U.S. Coast Guard at a boater's request. It invites other boaters to assist but is not a distress situation

marconi rig Uses tall triangular jib-headed sails instead of gaff rig; also called "Bermuda" rig. Most recreational vessels are now fitted with triangular shaped sails and are said to be "marconi-rigged"

marina A protected area offering various facilities required or desirable for recreational boats; also called a "yacht basin"

marine Of or relating to the sea

marine architect A person who designs ships; also may be called a "naval architect"

marine enamel Glossy finished paint designed to withstand the harsh marine environment

marine engine An internal combustion engine (gasoline or diesel) very similar to an automotive engine but with a few desirable modifications

mariner One who navigates or assists in navigating, seaman, sailor

marine railways Inclined planes at the water's edge on which vessels are "hauled out" of the water; also called "ways", "railways" or "slipways"

mariner's compass Compass used to navigate a vessel that has parallel magnetic needles or bundles of needles permanently attached to a card marked to indicate the direction and the degrees of a circle

marine sanitation devices MSDs, handle human waste

marine surveyor A person who inspects vessels to determine their overall condition

marine ways Inclined planes at the water's edge on which vessels are "hauled out" of the water; also called "ways", "railways" or "slipways"

marks The markings on a lead line

marl To wind or twist a small line around another

marline Light two-stranded line, used for lacings, whippings, seizings

marlinespike A pointed steel tool for splicing line

marlinespike seamanship The art of using line and making knots, bends, hitches and splices

marling The binding of two objects together

marling hitch A hitch used in marling

marry To join ropes by a worming over both

martingale A short, perpendicular spar, under the bowsprit end, used for guying the head-stays; also called the "dolphin-striker"

mast The principal vertical "spars" on which sails are set

before the mast *A person who has sailed on a fully rigged ship and lived in the crew's quarters which would be forward of the foremast*

by the board *When a vessel's masts fall over the side*

trim of masts *Their position in regard to the vessel and to each other*

undermasted *A vessel with masts of less than the usual dimensions*

mast band A band with fittings placed around the mast to which the stays, shrouds and tackle are fastened

mast boot Rubber or canvas waterproofing around the mast at the partners

mast cap A fitting on the top of the mast to which the stays, shrouds and halyards are fastened

mast coat An older name for waterproof material fitted around the foot of the mast to prevent water from entering between the mast and the deck; now called "mast boot"

masted Furnished with a mast or masts

master The commander of the vessel

masthead The top of the mast

masthead or pole compass A compass elevated above the deck in order to minimize the effect of the ship's attraction

masthead light A white light at the top of the mast

mast hoop A hoop for attaching a sail to a mast

mast or masting house Large building in which masts are made. May also have the equipment for stepping and unstepping masts

mastless Having no mast

mast partners Carlings (pieces of timber running between the beams) under the deck between the deck beams, where the mast passes through the deck, provides added strength to the deck in this area

mast step The base upon which the mast sets

mat Made from strands of old rope, used to prevent chafing

mate An officer ranking next to the master

matthew walker A stopper knot named after the originator

Mayday A radio distress call

mean sea level Average water level of the open ocean

mean tide range The range of tide, difference between high and low water

measurement The determination of "tonnage"; also called "admeasurement"

meridian A great circle on the surface of the earth passing through both poles, longitude is the distance east or west of Meridian of Greenwich

merriman clips A strong, quick opening and closing shackle often used with the spinnaker on small vessels

messenger A light line used to carry a heavier line from ship to the shore

metal threads A bolt which is threaded its entire length which normally has a round head with a screwdriver slot

MF (abbr) Medium frequency, radio

MHW (abbr) Mean high water

Microburst Mass of rapidly shifting, cold air spilling down from thunderstorm clouds at very high speeds; also called "upside-down tornado"

middle futtock timbers Timbers between the naval timbers and the top timbers

middle ground A shoal area located between two channels

midsea The open expanse of the sea

midship frame The largest rib which is also the first one set by the builder; the largest section of the frame

midship The middle of the ship between the bow and the stern and between port and starboard

midships The timbers at the broadest part of the vessel

mid-tide level Average water level offshore

Mike Used to indicate the letter "M"

mile A "statute mile," 5,280 feet

miles per hour (mph), statute mile, used on inland fresh water bodies

miss stays To fail on going about from one tack to another

mizzen Fore and aft sail set on the mizzen mast

mizzen mast The aftermost mast, the third mast from forward on vessels with three or more masts

model bow tug boat Typical tug with a pointed bow used primarily in towing

moderate breeze Wind having a speed of 13 to 18 mph

moderate gale Wind having a speed of 32 to 38 mph

monel A particularly good metal used in nails and screws on small boats, has great resistance to deterioration, approximately 60 to 70% nickel

monkey block Small single block strapped with a swivel

monkey fist Fancy knot often enclosing a weight, used on "heaving lines"

monkey island Navigation area on a large ship set above the bridge with a screening around most of its perimeter

monohull A vessel with a single hull

moonraker or moonsail A small sail sometimes carried in light winds, set at the top of the mast above the skysail on a square rigged ship

moorage Place for mooring

mooring A semi-permanent anchorage which has a buoy to which the vessel is secured

mooring bitt A post or cleat on the deck used to secure the anchor line or other lines

mooring buoy A buoy which has been anchored to the bottom and to which vessels may tie instead of anchoring

mooring lines Lines used to make a vessel fast to a shore structure; also called "dock lines"

mop A cloth broom used on board vessels

Morse code A system of "dots" and "dashes" sent by either sound or light which indicate various letters or numbers

motorboat A boat propelled by an internal combustion engine; also called "powerboats"

motor sailer A boat which has sails but less than most sailboats of similar size, has more engine power than a sailboat of similar size

moulded depth The distance between the keel and the top plank of the sides

moulds The patterns by which the frames of a vessel are worked out

mouse Turns of twine, taken across a hook, to prevent accidental unhooking; also called "mousing"

mouths Openings of rivers, creeks, harbors

MSD (abbr) Marine sanitation device

mud thrower Slang for power boats

muffle Putting mats or canvas around the looms in the row-locks

multihull Boat with more than one hull; catamaran, trimaran

multiple chines A vessel with more than one chine on each side which allows for a softer ride at high speeds, often called "deep-vee" design

multi-step hull One of the more complex hull designs

muscle boats Slang for high powered, recreational speed boats such as Cigarette boats

mushroom anchor An umbrella-shaped anchor which works very effectively in mud and sand, often used as a mooring anchor

NOVEMBER
N

N (abbr) North

napier diagram A graphic plot of compass deviation values

narrows The narrow section of a waterway

Nautical Almanac Annual publication containing tables of the positions of celestial bodies

nautical mile 6,076 feet

nautically After the manner of seamen or of the usages in seamanship

NAVAID A number of devices and systems which provide a navigator with data

naval architect An individual who prepares detailed plans and specifications for a vessel

naval Of or relating to ships and shipping

naval pipe The pipe through which the anchor line passes through the deck to the "chain locker"; also called "deck pipe" and "spurling pipe"

naval stores Turpentine, pitch, and rosin which get their name "naval stores" from when they were used extensively on wooden sailing vessels

naval timber Another name for ground futtock

navarchy Knowledge of managing ships

navicular Pertaining to a small ship or boat

naviculoid A small vessel

navigability State or condition of being navigable

navigable A safe area for navigation

navigableness Navigability

navigably In a navigable manner

navigate To steer, direct or manage a vessel underway

navigation lights Lights shown by a vessel to show position, course and use

navigation rules The rules of the road; governs such things as lights, sound signals, distress signals, meeting and passing of other vessels

navigation The art/science of safely guiding a vessel from one place to another

navigator One who navigates or is qualified to navigate

Navlights (abbr) Navigation lights

NE (abbr) Northeast

neap tides Occur during quarter moons, these tides have less range

neaped When a vessel is aground at the height of the spring tides; also called "beneaped"

near Close to the wind

neck That part of the oar where the "loom" (shaft) becomes the blade; also called the throat

nest When dories, or small boats, are stowed inside one another

net tonnage (Not net tons) The measurement of the earning power of the vessel when carrying cargo. Deduct the non-cargo carrying areas from the "gross tonnage"; also called "registered tonnage"

net tons A measurement of volume rather than weight

netting Network of line, used for stowing away sails or hammocks

nettles Small rope used for seizings and hammock clews; also called "knittles"

nip A short turn in a rope

noble metal A metal which is more capable in resisting deterioration from electrolysis than another, thus "leads" are often attached below the waterline to be sacrificed to electrolysis instead of the vessel's fittings made of brass or more "noble" metals

nock The forward upper end of a sail that sets with a boom

normal sheer When the deck slopes up toward the bow from amidships and the stern is at least level with amidships

Norman pin A round metal pin fitted horizontally through the head of a bitt or post in order to belay lines

norseman terminal A "swageless" method of attaching rigging wire to a rigging screw, design allows terminal to be screwed down hard onto the wire

northern cross Cross formed by the six stars in Cygnus

NOS (abbr) National Ocean Service

notice to mariners Official advices concerning navigational safety

November Used to indicate the letter "N"

numbering Federally mandated "licensing," usually done by the states. Boat numbers must be permanently attached to each side of the forward half of the vessel

numbers Slang for loran bearings of a particular place or object

nun Cylindrical red colored buoy, tapered toward the top

nut Projections on each side of the anchor shank, used to secure the stock to its place

NW (abbr) Northwest

nylon Synthetic material used to a great extent in rope

OSCAR
O

oakum Pieces of rope-yarns, used for caulking

oar Long wooden instrument with a flat blade, used for propelling boats

> ***bow oar*** *Foremost oar used in a boat except on a whaleboat where it is the second oar*

oarlock A "U"-shaped pivoting device in which oars are set when rowing; also called "rowlock"

oar stop A collar around the "loom" of an oar which is wider and thus prevents the oar from slipping out of the oarlock

occulting lights A light buoy which is lighted for longer periods of time than it is off, opposite of "flashing" light

ocean The vast body of water which covers more than two-thirds of the earth and which is divided in five parts—Atlantic, Pacific, Indian, Arctic and Antarctic Oceans

oceanfront Land which fronts on the ocean

ocean going Designed for travel on the ocean

ocean going tug boat Normally a deep draft vessel designed to operate hundreds of miles from the coast. Often will have only one propeller for fuel economy

oceanography The science of the ocean

off and on To stand on different tacks towards and from the land

offing Distance from the shore

offshore Some distance from the shore, often at least three miles

off-soundings When a vessel is too far from shore to take "soundings," normally considered to be the 100 fathom line

off the wind Sailing free with the yards eased off, when a sailboat has the wind astern; also called "sailing downwind," "running" and "free"

OHM A unit of electrical resistance

oil bag A soft container which holds oil and slowly disperses the oil onto the sea, calms the sea in the area of the oil

oil pressure alarm A warning alarm indicating low oil pressure in the engine

oil pressure gauge Indicates whether an engine is operating at a safe oil pressure in order to ensure proper lubrication

oil pump Supplies lubricants where necessary in the engine

oilskins Foul weather gear

Oily Waste Discharge Placard All vessels 26 ft. or longer must display it in the engine compartment, states the law and the penalty

old man The nickname which can be given to the captain of any large vessel

ombrometer A rain gauge

OMEGA A navigation system which electronically determines position

on beams-end Situation of a vessel when turned over, her beams inclined toward the vertical

one design class Boats of an identical design which race without a handicap

one part paints Paint which does not require mixing, used right out of the can as prepared

one shot method A method used in ferro-cement construction where the cement is pushed through the mesh and rods in one application instead of two

on shore On land or on land near the water

on-soundings When a vessel is not too far from shore to take "soundings," normally considered to be within the 100 fathom line

on the beam In line with the beams, at right angles with the keel

on the quarter In a direction considerably abaft of the beam, as the "wind is on the quarter"

on the wind Sailing into the wind with it as far ahead as possible; also called "close hauled," "to windward" or "beating"

open bollard A cleat with horns either side of an open center, center can be used as a fairlead

open boat A commercial fishing boat which takes individuals fishing for a fee with each individual paying their own fee. Usual trip is for 8 to 10 hours or less. Often called a "head boat." The opposite of a charter boat

open construction A vessel with no enclosed spaces

Oscar Used to indicate the letter "O"

outboard A boat propulsion unit attached at the transom

outboard cruiser A cruiser with outboard motor propulsion

outboard well A small cockpit just forward of the transom, allows an outboard motor to be hung on a low transom but the well keeps the water out of the boat

outdrive The motor is an inboard type motor mounted in the hull while the driving unit is external and similar to the lower section of an outboard engine; also called I/O, stern drive, inboard-outboard

outer jib A jib that is in front of the inner jib

outfoot To outsail another boat, normally used when both boats are sailing to the windward

outhaul A rope used for hauling out the clew of the sail

out of trim When a vessel's cargo is not stowed in such a way as to balance the vessel evenly

outpoint Sailing slightly closer to the wind than another boat

outrigger A spar rigged out to windward from the tops to spread the breast-backstays

outriggers (fish) Provides a pattern and separation of fishing lines to prevent snagging while trolling

overall length Measured from the fore part of the stem to the after part of stern along the centerline of the vessel, should not include any projections which are not part of the hull

overboard Goes over the side

overfall The disturbance, sometimes quite significant, of water rushing off a shoal area and falling into deeper water

overhand knot A very simple knot

overhang The projection of the upper part of the bow or stern beyond the point where the bow or stern intersects the waterline

overhaul a tackle To let go of the fall and pull on the leading parts in order to separate the blocks

overhead Same as a ceiling in a building, not to be confused with the "ceiling" on a boat which is the inside sides

overlap When the bow of an overtaking vessel passes the stern of the overtaken vessel

overtrimmed sails Sails are held in too tightly

oxidation Deterioration of an object starting on its surface due to its exposure to oxygen, normally called rust on iron

PAPA

P

packet A vessel which makes routine runs carrying mail, passengers and cargo

pad A slightly arched timber on top of the deck beam which gives the deck camber

paddle Similar to an oar but shorter with a wider blade, used vertically while being held in the hand

paddleboat Vessel propelled by a paddle wheel

paddle box Semicircular structure covering the upper portion of a paddle wheel

paddler Person who uses a paddle

paddle shaft Driving shaft of a paddle wheel

paddle steamer Steamboat with a paddle wheel instead of a propeller

paddle wheel Water wheel used to propel a steamboat

painter A towline for a dinghy or other small boat

palm 1. The broad tip of an anchor flute 2. A leather hand guard with a metal disk by the palm, used by sailmakers to push a needle through the sail

panting Stress on the hull from outside water pressure when the vessel pitches into head seas

pantry pump The pump used to provide fresh or salt water to the galley; also called "galley pump"

Papa Used to indicate the letter "P"

parallel rulers A navigation device, two rulers connected in parallel with linkages. By opening and "walking" them between an intended course and the chart's compass rose you can obtain the actual direction. Can also be used in reverse starting with the compass rose

paravane A triangular-shaped device with a fin (sometimes torpedo-shaped) towed on both sides of the vessel to increase stability

parbuckle To hoist or lower a spar or cask by single ropes around it

parcel To wrap tape around a wire or rope to prevent chafe

parral or parrel Ropes around the mast and through eyelets on the gaff sail to hold the sail to the mast; also called "jaw rope"

parrel trucks Wooden or plastic balls on the "parrel" which prevent it from binding on the mast

part To break a rope or chain

partners Framework fitted to the hole in a deck to receive the lower end of a mast

party boat A commercial fishing boat rented out on charter, often for sport fishing

passage 1. The act, the purchasable right or time consumed in traveling on board a vessel from one port to another, often construed to be of some distance 2. One leg of a voyage

work one's passage *Paying for passage by doing duty aboard a vessel*

patent log A towed device for measuring speed and distance

paunch mat A thick mat, placed at the slings of a yard

pawl A short bar, which prevents the capstan from turning back

pawl the capstan Set the pawls to prevent the capstan from recoiling

pay To "pay" is to cover over with tar or pitch

pay off When the vessel's head falls off from the wind

pay out To lessen the strain on a line and let it out slowly; also called "ease a line" and "veer out the cable"

pazaree Rope used for guying the clews out when before the wind

pea The very end of the palm of an anchor

peak The upper outer corner of a sail attached to a gaff

peak halyard The line that hoists the peak of a gaff

peak tanks Water tanks at either end of a vessel filled in order to trim the vessel

pelican hook A hinged hook with a sliding and locking collar, often used in gate openings of lifelines

pelorus A sighting device, without a compass, used to determine relative bearing

pendant or pennant 1. A line used to make a boat fast to a mooring buoy 2. A small flag, typically a signal flag

period of wave Time between crests

personal flotation device Any of several types of items such as life vests, rings or seat cushions

PFD (abbr) Personal flotation device

pier Structure extending into the water, used as a landing place for vessels

pierage Charge for using a marine pier

pierhead The outer extremity of a pier which forms the landing place

pile Vertical wooden pole driven into the water's bottom

pile driving When a vessel continuously lifts its "forefoot" out of the water and slams down with each consecutive wave

piling A structure of piles

pillow A block which supports the inner end of the bowsprit

pilot An individual authorized to take large ships in and out of restricted waters such as rivers and harbors when the Captain may not be completely knowledgeable in the area

pilot boat Boat which carries the pilot from the shore to the ship he will be piloting

pilothouse A deckhouse for the helmsman and navigation equipment

piloting Navigation using visual references, the depth of the water and similar known information

pilot waters Waterways where the use of a pilot is required

pin Axis on which a sheave turns

pinch To hold a sailboat so close to the wind that the sails lose efficiency and shiver; also called "pinching"

pink stern When a vessel has a high, narrow stern, pointed at the end

pinnace Boat in size between a launch and a cutter

pin rail A rail, often supported by the shrouds, with holes used to hold belaying pins in an upright position

pintle Metal bolt, used for hanging a rudder

pipe deck filler A flush fitting with a flush cap connected by pipe to tanks below the deck; also called "deck filler" and "filler"

pitch The alternate rise and fall of the bow while proceeding through waves

pitch of propeller Theoretical distance a vessel would advance with one revolution of the propeller. Thus an 18 ft. by 16 ft. propeller would have a diameter of 18 ft. and propel the boat 16 ft. with one revolution

pitch of rivets Distance between rivets

pitch pole When a boat is thrown end-over-end into the rough seas

planing hull A hull designed so that forward speed creates water lift

planks Lengths of wood used for external skin or deck; also called "planking"

plank sheer Timber carried around a vessel's hull for securing the timber-heads, the covering board

pledge Oakum ready to be used for caulking

plimsoll line Markings on the side of a ship indicating the safe limit of cargo which may be loaded; also called "load line"

plow anchor Lightweight anchor (CQR), holds well but hard to stow

plug A piece of wood, fitted into a hole, to keep water in or out

plumb bow or plumb stem When the stem of the vessel is perpendicular to the waterline

plummer block A shaft bearing whose housing bolts to a horizontal surface

point To take the end of a rope and work it over with knittles

point of departure Last fixed position obtained by outward-bound vessel

points of the compass The thirty-two points of direction into which the compass card of a mariner's compass is divided

point system A traditional system using 32 points of a compass to indicate the direction of an object, today we may be more inclined to use the clock system

pole Applied to highest mast of a ship

pole or masthead compass A compass elevated above the deck in order to minimize the effect of the ship's attraction

polyester Synthetic material which is stronger with less elasticity than nylon, used in rope and sails

polypropylene Lightweight synthetic material used in lines where flotation is desirable

poop A raised deck over the after part of the spar deck

poop cabin Cabin built under the poop-deck

poop-deck Deck built over a cabin of a ship, when the cabin is on the spar deck

pooped Struck on the poop by a heavy sea

pooping 1. Shock of a heavy sea on the stern of a vessel 2. The action of one vessel running into the stern of another

poop lantern A light signal carried on a vessel's taffrail

poppets Perpendicular pieces of timber fixed to the fore-and-aft part of the bilgeways when launching a vessel

pop rivet A specially designed rivet which can be inserted and expanded from one side when there is not access to both sides

port 1. The left side of the boat 2. An opening in a vessel's side for air and light or drain water from the deck 3. The harbor and all the harbor's facilities

port bar A bar used to secure the ports of a vessel

porthole Window

porthook One of the hooks in the side of a vessel to which the hinges of a port-lid are hooked

portlight The glass used in a porthole when the porthole can be opened

port of call 1. Port where vessels normally stop for supplies and repairs 2. A stop included on an itinerary

portoise Gunwale of the vessel as used in the term "a portoise"

> *lower the yards "a portoise"* Lower the yards to the gunwale

> *ride "a portoise"* To have the lower yards and topmasts struck or lowered when at anchor in a gale

port quarters Port side of a vessel, from amidships to the stern

port tack A sailing vessel with the wind coming from the port (left) side

position finding A navigational process of determining the location of a vessel

pound A boat in heavy seas which comes down hard with successive waves

powerboats Also called motorboats, one of the basic divisions of boats based on their propulsion

power converter Converts 120 volt AC shore power into lower voltage DC to charge and prevent batteries from becoming discharged; also called "battery charger"

power wash High velocity, hand held water sprayer used to wash bottoms of boats when they are hauled from the water

pram A small boat used as a tender, a dinghy with squared-off bow

pratique Permission to land in a foreign port after clearance by medical officers

prayer book A small, flat holystone, used to clean wooden decks in narrow places

preventer A contrivance of rope, spar, cable and the like used to secure bracing, such as a preventer stay on a mainmast, an additional rope or spar, used as a support

pricker A small marling spike, used in sail-making, rigging and the like

Prime Meridian Longitudinal line which passes through Greenwich, England which is designated 0 degrees

privileged vessel Vessel having the right of way

prolonged blast Sounding the vessel's horn or other sound device for a few seconds

propeller A rotating device that propels a vessel; sometimes called a "wheel" or a "screw"

propeller shaft Connects the engine to the propeller in order to turn the propeller; also just called "shaft"

propulsion Three basic types of propulsion used in boats—motor, sail and row

protractor Navigational device used to measure and lay down angles on a chart

prow The bow

psychrometer Weather instrument, with a dry and wet bulb, to measure moisture

pudden fender A thick fender fitted on the bow, type often used on tug boats

puddening A quantity of yarns, matting or oakum used to prevent chafing

pulpit 1. An extension on a powerboat, forward of the bow, normally consisting of a small platform with rails extending around it 2. Bow rail installations on a sailboat whether they extend forward of the bow or not

pump A device designed to move, raise or compress various liquids

pump brake The handle to the pump

pump well A well containing the bilge pump into which even small amounts of water will drain

punt A small shallow draft boat propelled by a pole being pushed against the bottom of the waterway

purchase A device for obtaining a mechanical advantage, a "block and tackle"

push boat Normally a tug boat with a blunt bow used to push barges and other vessels

pusher tug boat A tug boat designed with a blunt bow used primarily in pushing barges and other other vessels; may be called "push boats"

pushpits An extension on a sailboat similar to a "pulpit" on a motorboat

put about Go on opposite tack; also said "go about"

QUEBEC

Q

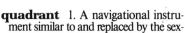

quadrant 1. A navigational instrument similar to and replaced by the sextant 2. The fitting on top of the rudder stock shaped like a quarter of a circle to which the steering cable is attached

quadrant throttle A quarter of a circle shaped throttle control with a serrated side which holds the control lever at a desired setting

quarantine Square yellow flag

quarter 1. The side of a vessel, from amidships to the stern 2. Quarter of the yard is between the slings and the yard-arm

broad on the port quarter Direction midway between "dead astern" and "abeam" on the port side

broad on the starboard quarter Direction midway between "dead astern" and "abeam" on the starboard side

on the quarter In a direction considerably abaft of the beam, as the wind was on the quarter

quarterbadge An ornament on the quarters of a vessel

quarter berth A berth in a quarter of the vessel

quarterbitt Stout post on a vessel's deck used for mooring and towing

quarter-block A block set under the quarters of a yard for the clewlines and sheets to reeve through

quarterboard One of the boards raising the bulwarks of the quarter; a top-gallant bulwark

quarter-boat Boat hanging by davits on a vessel's quarters

quarterdeck Upper deck abaft the mainmast

quarter fast A rope by which the quarter of a vessel is secured to a dock or pier

quarter galley Balcony on a ship's quarter which may extend over the stern

quartering Sailing with the wind over the side of a vessel, from amidships to the stern

quartermaster A petty officer, who attends the helm, binnacle and similar bridge duties

quarter netting Netting hung along the quarter rails of older vessels for the storage of hammocks

quarter piece One of several pieces of timber near the taffrail at the after-part of the quarter-gallery

quarter point A fourth part of the distance between any two points of the mariner's compass

quarter rail That part of the rail from the stern to the gangway guarding the quarterdeck

quarters Side of a vessel, from amidships to the stern

quarter-sling A sling on either side of the center of a yard to support it

quarter-timbers One of the timbers in the quarter

quarter-watch One-half of the watch is on duty

quarterwind A wind which blows on the vessel's quarter

quay A masonry structure at the water's edge, where vessels may tie up

Quebec Used to indicate the letter "Q"

quick-work The vessel's sides above the chainwales and decks

quilting A coating outside of the vessel made from rope woven together

ROMEO
R

rabbet A grove into which an edge of a plank is inserted

race A strong and rapid current through a narrow channel or in a small area of the sea

rack 1. To seize lines together with cross-turns 2. A "fair-leader"

rack a tackle To bind together two ropes of a tackle to prevent the ropes from reeving back through the blocks

rack-bar Piece of wood used to twist the bight of a rope, called a swifter, in order to bind together the parts of a raft

rack block A block for "running rigging" which contains a number of sheaves

racking When two structural members are trying to work independently of one another even though they are attached

racking seizing A seizing which is a series of figure-eights, designed to dampen the racking moment between the standing part of the rope and the tail

radar An electronic device that shows position and size of another object on its screen

radar reflector A diamond-shaped metal device hung on the rigging to increase visibility on another vessel's radar

radio beacon A transmitter at a known location used by vessels to determine their positions

radio bearing A direction determined by the source of a radio transmission

radio direction finder A receiver which determines the direction to the source of radio waves

radio log Not normally required but often a good idea, especially on events that could lead to legal action. Compulsorily equipped vessels must maintain such a log

radionavigation Electronic piloting

raffee A triangular sail set above the highest yard of a square-rigged vessel

rafting Mooring procedure used by two or more vessels tied side-by-side

rag bolt A rough nail with a jagged shank which prevents the nail from working itself out of a plank or a timber

rail A protective edge on deck, the top of the bulwarks if they exist

railways Inclined planes at the water's edge on which vessels are "hauled out" of the water; also called "marine ways" or "ways"

raise When something becomes visible

raised deck cruiser The cabin is formed by extending the topsides above the deck level and not allowing any side walkways

raised head screw A regular wood screw designed so that the head will remain above the surface for easier, future removal

rake or raked The slant of a ship's funnels, bow, stern or mast

raked bow or stem The stem of the vessel is inclined at an angle to the waterline

ramline A line used in making masts in order to get a straight middle line on a spar

range Two objects which are in line and used as an aid in steering a course

range of cable A quantity of cable, ready for letting go the anchor or paying out

range of tide The difference in the height between high tide and low tide

ratchet block A block on which the sheave is controlled by a ratchet, which prevents it from going in the opposite direction

rat guard Conical shaped metal placed on the dock lines in order to prevent rats from coming aboard

rating rule A system of handicapping in sailboat racing

ratlines Horizontal lines running across the shrouds that are used as a ladder

rattle-down rigging Putting "ratlines" upon the rigging

raw water cooled Using the outside water on which the boat is floating to cool the engine

raw water flow alarm Warning alarm indicating inadequate cooling system water

RDF (abbr) Radio direction finder

reach Sailing with the wind on or forward of the beam; also called "tacking to the windward" and "reaching"

ready about Order to "stand by" in preparation to tacking the vessel; also called "about ship"

reciprocal Going in the opposite direction

recirculating toilets Normally portable, they contain a few gallons of water and chemicals. The waste and the treated water are "recirculated" each time it is used and should be emptied in several days

red lead A primer paint of lead oxide and linseed oil

reduction gear Gears used to lower the speed of a propeller to a rate slower than the engine which increases efficiency

reef 1. To shorten sail by reducing the area exposed 2. An underwater barrier such as coral or rock

shake out a reef To let out a reef thus enlarging the sail area

reef band A band of canvas sewn on the sail to be used for reefing the sail

reef cringle Hook-shaped device which snares the grommets on the luff of the sail

reef earing A short length of rope used to haul down and secure the reef cringle

reefer A person who reefs sails, specifically a midshipman in the past

reef jig A small tackle used to make the reef-band taut before knotting the points in

reef knot The knot used to tie a reef, a square knot

reef points Tie lines which reduce the sail area when tied around the foot of the sail

reef tackle Used to haul out the foot of the sail

reef tie Same as reef-point

reeve To pass a line through a hole or a block; also called "rove"

registered boats All machinery-propelled vessels except racing boats and tenders under 10 hp must be registered with the state of principal use or with the U.S. Coast Guard

registered tonnage (Not net tons) The measurement of the earning power of the vessel when carrying cargo. Deduct the non-cargo carrying areas from the "gross tonnage"; also called "net tonnage"

registration The numbering or licensing of a boat

relative bearing A direction in relation to the fore-and-aft line of a vessel

relieving tackle Tackle connected to the tiller and used for steering in the event of a failure in the normal steering system

render 1. To pass a rope through an object 2. Ensure that a line will pass freely through a hole or a block; also called "render a line"

reverse gears Changes the direction of the rotation of the propeller

reverse sheer Deck slopes down towards the bow and/or the stern from amidships

reversing tidal current Normal tidal current which flows in one direction and then the opposite, unlike "rotary tidal currents"

revolutions per minute RPM, the speed at which an engine is turning

rhumb line Straight line used in laying out a course

ribband carvel A method used in building a wooden vessel in which the fore and aft planks are butted together, flush on all edges and rove down on inside battens; also called "batten carvel"

rib-bands Narrow and flexible timber nailed to the outside of the ribs, the length of the vessel

ribbing-nail Nail with a large round head with a ring to prevent the head from splitting the timber or from being drawn through, used mainly for fastening rib-bands; also called "ribband" nails

ribs The skeleton of a vessel which is wood set into the keel at a right angle and which are then covered with planking; also called "frames"

ride an anchor To lie at anchor

ride a portoise To have the lower yards and topmasts struck or lowered when at anchor in a gale

ride at anchor Same as "at anchor," a vessel when she rides by her anchor or is anchored

ride down the sail To bear down by strength and weight on the sail

ride out To withstand the fury of a storm

ridge rope A line used to support an awning

riding bitts Stout vertical posts to which lines are belayed when they are subject to heavy strains; also called bitts

riding light The anchor light

riding sail Three-cornered sail fastened to the mainmast and sheeted down aft; used to steady a vessel when head on to the wind

rig The arrangement of a sailboat's mast and sails

rigger 1. A person who rigs vessels 2. A ship of a specific rig such as a "square-rigger"

rigging All the lines which secure and control the sails, masts and spars on a sailboat

set up rigging *Means to tighten rigging*

rigging loft Room used to prepare rigging for vessels

rigging screw Another name for "turnbuckle"; also called "bottle screw"

right a vessel Restore the vessel to an upright position after careening

right hand lay Stranded rope with a twist towards the right; also called "right hand rope"

right hand propeller A propeller which turns to the right (clockwise) when it is viewed from the stern

right hand rope Right twist on stranded rope; also called "right hand lay"

right of way A vessel which has priority when meeting another

right the helm Center the steering wheel

ring The iron ring at the top of the anchor to which the cable is connected

ring bolt An eye-bolt with a ring through the eye which is fastened to the deck or side, used for hooking tackle

ring buoy Ring-shaped flotation device, normally has a grab line attached at four points

ringsail Same as "ringtail"

ringtail A small sail used in light winds, shaped like a jib and set abaft the spanker, same as "ringsail"

riparian right A right of one owning land under the the water, riparian land

rips Short, steep waves caused by currents meeting

rise When coming near another ship, it appears above the horizon

rising line Parts of a vessel's floor where the floor timbers terminate upon the lower futtock; also called "dead rising"

risings Stringers placed in a boat for the support of the thwarts

roach A curve in the foot of a square sail by which the clews are brought below the middle of the foot

road or roadstead An anchorage some distance from the shore

roaring forties A belt of prevailing and strong westerly winds south of latitude 40 degrees

roband Short lengths of rope which attach the headrope of a squaresail to the jackstay; also called "ropeband" and "robbin"

rockered When a keel viewed from the side is not straight

rocket launchers Fishing rod holders that point upwards and backwards, normally in groups of three to six

rode The anchor line

rod holders May be located in various places on a boat. A short tube-like device large enough to hold the handle of a fishing rod. May be placed individually or in series around the boat either attached to a supporting frame or set into the gun'l

roll Alternating motion of a boat, port and starboard

roller fairlead Fairlead which includes a roller for the cable such as an anchor roller

roller furling Method of furling sail by winding it onto a stay

roller reefing Reduction of the sail area by winding the sail onto a rotating boom

rolling chock or cleat Secondary external keels at the turn of the bilge which helps reduce a vessel's roll, normally on larger round-bottom vessels; also called "bilge keels"

rolling hitch A knot useful for attaching a line to another line or to a spar

rolling tackle Tackle used to steady the yards during heavy seas

rolling topsail A topsail which may be taken in around a roller which is located under the sail

Romeo Used to indicate the letter "R"

rooming Increasing the distance off the lee shore to ensure that the wind does not jeopardize the safety of a vessel

rooves Copper washers used with copper nails inside a wooden boat

rooving iron Device used to hold a roove in place over the end of a nail

rope Cordage of fiber or steel, normally called "lines" aboard a ship

ropeband Short, flat plaited rope with an eye in one end, used in pairs to tie the upper edges of square sails to their yards; also called "robbin" and "roband"

rope locker A storage compartment for the anchor chain; also called "cable locker" and "chain locker"

rope-yarn The basic ingredient of rope

rotary tidal currents Unlike normal tidal currents, there is little change in strength. These currents, which may occur off shore, slowly and steadily, change direction

rotate the watch Changing the persons on "watch"

rough log The deck log (see deck log)

rough-tree An unfinished spar

round bottom One of the three basic bottom shapes—flat, round and vee

round head screw A wood screw with a head shaped like a half of a sphere

roundhouse A cabin in the after part of a vessel having the "poop" for its roof. The old name for this would be the "coach", which was the Captain's quarters

round in To haul in a rope

rounding 1. Small rope or yarn wound around a larger rope or spar; also called service 2. The act of turning in course, as the rounding of a vessel in landing

round seizing A seizing used when the strain on both rope ends is in the same direction

round top Platform at the masthead

round turn 1. A turn of line around an object or a line 2. Part of a knot

round turn and two half hitches A turn of a line around an object and then finished with two half hitches, a simple and effective knot when tying to an object

round up To haul up on a tackle

rove To pass a line through a hole or opening; also called "reeve"

row Propelling a boat with oars

> *catch a crab* *To catch an oar in the water by feathering it too soon*

> *lay on oars* *Stop rowing*

rowboat A light craft propelled by one or more persons using oars, one of the basic divisions of boats based on their propulsion

rowlock "U"-shaped pivoting device in which oars are set when rowing; also called "oarlock"

royal Sail next above the top-gallant sail

royal mast A mast above the top-gallant mast and below the skysail mast

royal yard Fourth yard from the deck from which the "royal" is set

RPM (abbr) Revolutions per minute, speed of the engine

rubber Device used to flatten down the seams of a sail in sail-making

rubbing strake Heavy strake in the topsides which extends beyond the face of the other planking. Used to protect a vessel as would a rub rail; also called a "rubbing piece." Not the same as a rub rail which is a strip of wood added externally

rubrail Strip added to the outer side of vessel's topsides to absorb friction from pilings and docks

rudder Pivoted flat surface, on a vertical axis, in the water, at or near the stern which controls the direction of the vessel

rudder angle indicator Shows the exact position of the rudder on the instrument's gauge

rudder-chain Linked and running from the rudder to the quarters (port and starboard in the stern of a vessel), used to prevent the rudder from being lost if unshipped, not normally used on modern vessels

rudder coat Piece of canvas or other material put around the rudderhead to keep the sea from coming in at the tiller hole

rudderhead Upper end of the rudder into which the tiller is fitted

rudderhole Hole through which the head of the rudder passes

rudderless A vessel which has lost it's rudder

rudder pendant A continuation of the rudder chain

rudderpost Upper extension of the rudder to which pressure is applied in order to turn the rudder

rudder stock The axle on which the rudder turns and the rudder plate is attached

rudder trunk The casing through which the rudder stock enters the vessel

rule of sixty A piloting technique that provides a simple method of clearing an obstacle with little chart work

rules of the road Regulations used in order to prevent collisions (Colregs)

rumboline Worn

run 1. The after part of a vessel's bottom which narrows and rises as it approaches the stern-post, the vessel's lines aft of the stern 2. Course or distance sailed by a vessel 3. A voyage, trip or passage from one port to another

runabouts A broad classification of motor boat normally used for day fishing or recreational outings

rung-heads The upper ends of the floor timbers

runner A rope used to increase the effectiveness of tackle when "blocks and tackle" are arranged in a specific manner

runners Set up on either side of the boom and attached to the mast to help balance the strain placed on the backstay; also called "running backstays"

running or running free When a sailboat has the wind astern; also called "sailing downwind," "off the wind," "free"

by the run Let a vessel go without attempting to slack off

running backstays See "runners"

running bowline A bowline tied around the same line in order to form a noose

running fix Two bearings are taken on the same object for a navigational triangle

running lights The required navigational lights used during periods of low visibility

running part Any line on a tackle which moves as compared to any stationary line attached to the block or an object. The stationary line is called the "standing part"

running rigging The adjustable lines used to control spars and sails

running sail Sail adapted to downwind sailing such as the spinnaker and drifter

running stay A stay which can be adjusted according to the wind conditions, normally a backstay

SIERRA
S

S (abbr) South

S-twist Term for left-hand-lay rope

saddles Pieces of wood hollowed out to fit on the yards. A hollow in the upper part is a rest for the boom

safe working load (SWL) The load limit at which any tackle may be used safely

safety harness Should be worn by all crew members on sailboats during rough weather. Made of rope or webbing with snap-type hooks for fast connection to rigging and life lines

sag To drift, to "sag" to the leeward, to drift off to leeward

sagged When a vessel droops amidships

sail 1. Propulsion devices on some boats 2. To be conveyed on a boat, such as "set sail," "sailed upon" 3. To direct or manage the movement of a vessel

blooper sail Secondary running sail hoisted with the spinnaker

loose sails Unfurl the sails

ride down the sail To bear down by strength and weight on the sail

riding sail Three-cornered sail fastened to the mainmast and sheeted down aft; used to steady a vessel when head on to the wind

set sail To raise the sail; to leave the harbor

shake out the sails Cause the sails to flap by bringing the bow into the wind

shorten sail Take in canvas to reduce the sail area

shoulder of mutton sail Triangular sail used chiefly to set on a boat's mast

spring a luff To yield to the helm and sail nearer to the wind

strike sail To lower the sails suddenly

suit of sails Sailboat's complete set of sails

take in Lower the sails

trim of sails The position and arrangement of sails best suited for a particular vessel in propelling it forward

under sail With the sails spread

sailable Navigable

sailboard A small flat sailboat that is designed for one or two passengers

sailboat antenna Name often used for the basic VHF antenna since it is primarily used on a masthead

sailboats One of the basic divisions of boats based on their propulsion, a boat which is moved by sails

sailborne Borne or conveyed by sails

sail burton Tackle used for hoisting sails aloft

sail close to the wind Sailing with the vessel's head so near to the wind as to fill the sails without shaking them

sailcloth Heavy canvas used for sails and the synthetic material more commonly used today

sail cover Covers placed over the sails when not being used

sailer Ship or a boat having specified sailing qualities

sail fine Sail close to the wind

sail free Sailing somewhat further from the wind than when close hauled

sail-ho! Cry when a sail is spotted at sea

sailing 1. A sport 2. A departure from a port 3. The skill of managing and navigating a vessel

sailing charts Smallest scale charts which cover large areas of a coastline. Used when approaching shore from the open ocean or when cruising between distant points

sailing downwind When a sailboat has the wind astern; also called "running," "off the wind," "free"

sailing master The navigation officer on a vessel; a navigator

sail less Without sails

sail loft A building with a large open area in which sails are made and serviced

sailmaker Knowledgeable and experienced person who makes sails

sailmaker's needle Available in different sizes, good for making whippings and minor repairs to the sail and its attachments

sailmaker's palm Leather glove which protects the hand's palm while pushing a sailmaker's needle through something being sewn or whipped

sailmaker's whipping The best method of whipping

sailmaking The art and/or business of making sails

sailor A person who sails aboard any ship

sailorman Seaman, sailor

sail panels Pieces cut obliquely and put into the sail to add breadth to a sail; also called "goring-cloths"

sail room Compartment on a vessel for stowage of sails not in use

sail ticklers Yarn sewn into the leading edge of the sail which can indicate the flow of wind in this area of greatest lift

sail track The track on the aft of the mast in which the track slides of the sail are attached

sail yard Yard or spar on which sails are extended

salinity Salty, the amount of dissolved salt in the water

saloon The lounging area aboard a small boat

salty An individual or thing obviously from on or around the sea

sampson post 1. Single bitt forward used to fasten the anchor line of a small boat 2. On larger boats it is the small forward derrick mast, used with the cargo boom

sandbagger A boat, normally from earlier times, that used sand bags for ballast

sandbank A shoal in a waterway caused by sand collecting in the area

SAR (abbr) Search and rescue

sash eye Small eye attached to a plate which can be screwed onto the deck; also called "deck eye"

satellite navigation Allows the forming of a position using radio transmissions from satellites

save-all A small sail, often called a catch-all

saxboard An open boat's "sheer strake," which is the top board

scantling Term applied to any timber when reduced to standard size

scantlings The measurements of the structural members of a vessel

scarf Method of joining together two members where the joint is cut at a significant angle or otherwise elongated by shaving or notching the two members

scend The rising of the bow when the stern falls into a trough

schooner Fore-and-aft rigged vessel, two to six masts, foremast shorter than main

scope 1. The ratio of the amount of anchor line used to the distance to the bottom of the water as measured from the deck of the boat 2. Sometimes used to refer to the amount of anchor cable in use

score A groove in a block

Scotch mist A light and misty rain; some call it an "Irish Mist"

scotchman A large batten placed over the turnings-in of rigging, to prevent chafing

scow A barge-like vessel with a flat bottom and square ends

scraper Small, triangular iron instrument with a handle used for scraping decks, masts and other areas

screw A propeller; sometimes called a wheel

screw alley A tunnel on larger vessels through which the propeller shaft passes. Separates the shaft area from other compartments and provides a working area in which to service the shaft

scrowl A piece of timber bolted to the knees of the head, used instead of a figure-head

scud or scudding 1. To drive before a gale with little or no sail 2. When a sailboat has the wind astern, may be called "sailing downwind," "off the wind," "free"

scull or sculling Propelling a rowboat while standing and using one oar over the stern

scupper Drainhole in the bulwarks or toe rail which allows water to run overboard from the deck; also called "freeing port"

scuttle 1. A hole cut in a vessel's deck such as a hatchway 2. A hole cut in any part of the vessel 3. "To scuttle" is to cut holes in the vessel or open sea cocks in order to make her sink

scuttlebutt 1. A cask with a hole cut in its bilge and kept on deck to hold water 2. Rumors and gossip which the sailors use to get while gathered around the scuttlebutt drinking water

SE (abbr) Southeast

sea 1. Waves in a specific area caused by blowing wind 2. A general term used to describe the water action on the surface

heavy sea When the surface of a body of water is broken into a number of large waves

sea acorn A barnacle

sea anchor Open ended canvas cone used to slow the downwind drift of a boat in heavy weather and/or to keep the bow of the boat into the wind; also called a "drogue"

seabag Cylindrical canvas bag used for clothes and other gear

sea bank 1. The seashore 2. A man-made bank to protect the land from the sea

seabeach A beach lying along the seacoast

seabed The floor of the ocean or sea

sea biscuit Hard biscuit, bread or below average food which may be used on ships

sea board 1. Seacoast 2. The country bordering on a seacoast

sea boat Vessel capable of operating in heavy seas

seaboot A waterproof boot often used by sailors

seaborne Borne over or upon the sea

seabound Bounded by the sea

sea bow Marine rainbow

sea boy A boy employed on a vessel

sea bread Below average food, "hardtack"

sea breeze A light wind from the sea blowing ashore

sea built Built for or by the sea

sea cap The crest of a wave, the whitecap

sea captain The master, normally of a commercial vessel

sea card Card in a mariner's compass

sea chest Storage chest for personal property

seacoast Land, shore or community bordering the sea

sea cocks A through-hull valve just inside the "through-hull" fitting where water is taken in or discharged for the engine cooling, waste disposal, and the like; a safety device

sea compass Mariner's compass

seacraft 1. Seagoing vessels 2. Skill in navigation

seadog A veteran sailor

seadrome An airdrome on the water

seafarer Mariner

seafaring A mariner's calling in life

sea fire Phosphorescence in the sea

seafloor Seabed

sea foam Froth or foam often seen on the sea

seafront Waterfront of a seaside place

sea froth Same as "sea foam"

sea gate 1. A channel or way giving access to the sea 2. Long rolling wave or swell

sea gauge Depth that a vessel sinks into the water

seagirt Surrounded by the sea

seagoing Ocean going

sea kindly Comfortable in rough seas

sea ladder A rope ladder or steps lowered over the side of a vessel

sea-lane An established sea route

sea language The salty slang and terms used by seamen

sea lawyer A hard to please, argumentative seaman

sea legs Being able to comfortably walk aboard a vessel while it is being tossed about and not becoming seasick

sealer The individual or the vessel engaged in seal hunting

sea level The level of the surface of the sea especially at its mean position midway between mean high and low water

seaman Anyone who puts to sea

seamanlike Characteristics of a competent seaman

seamanly See "seamanlike"

seamanship All the arts and skills of boat handling

seamark 1. A line on the coast marking the tidal limit 2. An elevated object serving as a beacon

sea mile A nautical mile, 6,076 feet

seams Intervals between planks on side or the deck

sea mud Rich saline deposits or soft mud from salt marshes near the seashore; also called "ooze"

sea ooze See "sea mud"

seaport Port, harbor or town having access to the sea

seaquake An earthquake at sea

sea rat Pirate or sea-thief

sea risk Hazard or risk at sea

sea robber A pirate

sea room Having an adequate size area in which to navigate a vessel

sea rover A pirate, one who roves the sea

seashore Land adjacent to the sea, seacoast

seasickness A motion sickness from being on the water

seaside Land adjacent to the sea

sea smoke Widespread and dense fog caused by cold winter air blowing off the land and across the adjacent coastal water

seasonal buoys In areas of severe icing, normal buoys will be removed during the winter for their protection and may be replaced with "ice buoys"

sea steps Projecting metal bars or steps attached to the side of a vessel for use in boarding

sea stores Supplies, including food, put aboard and required for a voyage

seastrand The seashore

sea term Words or terms used by seamen particularly in navigation

sea thief A pirate

seatrain A ferry-like ship on which railroad trains are carried across bodies of water

sea turn Wind or breeze from the sea which is normally followed by inclement weather

sea valve A sea cock through the vessel's hull

seawall A wall or embankment built to protect the shore from erosion or to act as a breakwater

seaward Toward the sea

seaway 1. Moderate or rough seas 2. A vessel's headway 3. Waterway to the ocean

seaworthy Vessel is in sufficient enough condition to handle the perils of the sea

secret fastened deck A deck on which no fastening nails or screws show. Planks are nailed on an angle from the side plus nailed through the side to the adjacent plank

sedan cruiser Main cabin is on the same level as the after cockpit and opens onto the cockpit

seize To fasten ropes together or rope to a spar (light lines)

seized Wrapping twine or thread around a line to prevent it from untwisting; also called "whipped"

self-aligning stuffing box A stuffing box mounted by a rubber or flexible tube

self bailer A tube often found in the stern of small power boats. When the plug is removed while under motion, it allows the boat to drain safely by a "venturi" action

self tailing winch Line coming off the winch is secured through a type of a cam cleat which prevents the line from slipping back

selvagee Skein of rope-yarns marled together. Used as a neat strap

sennit Braid formed by plaiting rope-yarns together; also called "sinnit"

sentinel A weight sent halfway down the anchor rode to lower the angle of pull on the anchor; also known as a "kellet"

serve or serving To wind small stuff around a line in order to prevent chafing

serve the cable To bind it round with ropes, canvas or anything which will prevent it from being worn in the hawse

serving mallet A mallet used in serving a rope. The mallet is rotated around the rope with the marline feeding off and serving it

set Direction in which a current flows

set and drift Direction and distance a current travels during a specific time

set bolt A pin used to hold planks firmly together

set sail 1. To raise the sail 2. To leave the harbor

settee rig A four-sided sail with a spar holding the upper side; also called "gaff rig"

set the land To see how the land bears from the vessel by using a compass

setting pole A long pole which may be iron-pointed, used for pushing boats along in shallow water

set up rigging Tighten rigging

sewed Condition of a ship when she is high and dry on the shore; same as sued

sextant Used to sight on various celestial bodies such as the the sun, moon, stars, planets which are then used with various charts to determine position

shackle A "U"-shaped link in a chain with a movable bolt so chain can be separated. Used to connect anchor lines, fasten blocks; also called "clevis"

shackle key A flat, slotted tool used to loosen and tighten shackles, often has a bottle opener and a can opener at either end

shaft Connects the engine to the propeller in order to turn the propeller; also called "propeller shaft"

shaft alley or tunnel A tunnel on larger vessels through which the propeller shaft passes. Separates the shaft area from other compartments and provides a working area in which to service the shaft

shaft log Device on a boat through which the propeller shaft passes. The "stuffing box" at this point prevents water leakage

shake a vessel in the wind To luff a vessel until her upper sails shake

shakedown cruise First cruise of the vessel in order to correct any problems or the first cruise with its crew in order to develop efficiency

shake out a reef To let out a reef, thus, enlarging the sail area

shake out the sails Cause the sails to flap by bringing the bow into the wind

shallow-bodied Vessel with a shallow hold

shamrock knot Also called a "jury mast knot" since it is often used to take the stays and shrouds of a temporarily rigged mast

shank The main piece in an anchor (center piece)

shank-painter Rope securing the anchor's shank to the ship's side

sharp up Yards when braced as near fore-and-aft as possible

sharpie Vessel with an abrupt angle where the bottom and the topsides meet at a well-defined area, "hard chined"

shear hulk Old vessels fitted with "shears" and used for changing spars of other vessels. These would not be very common in this day of age; also spelled "sheer hulk"

shear pin Relatively soft pin which is part of the propeller assembly. The pin breaks when the propeller strikes something hard thus preventing serious damage to the engine

shears Two spars, raised at angles and lashed, used for hoisting; also spelled "sheers"; see "sheer legs"

sheathing Covering formally used on ship's wooden bottom as protection from worms, usually thin plates of copper or an alloy containing copper

sheave Grooved wheel over which a rope runs, often part of blocks

sheep shank Hitch used to temporarily shorten rope

sheer 1. Curvature of the deck, fore and aft, as seen from the side 2. A turn, deviation or change of course 3. Position of a vessel riding to a single anchor and heading toward it

sheer batten Long strip of wood nailed to the ribs, in shipbuilding used to show the position of the wales or bends before bolting on the planks

sheer hulk In former times, an old ship cut down to the lower deck and fitted with sheers to fix or take out masts of other ships; also spelled "shear hulk"

sheer legs Two poles lashed together at the top from which tackle is hung and with the bottoms separated, used as a support in order to lift heavy objects

sheer pole 1. One of the legs of a sheers 2. A rod lashed to the shrouds just above the dead-eyes to prevent the shrouds from turning

sheer rail Lowest plank of the "bulwarks" which is the wood work around a vessel above the deck

sheer strake Topmost plank on the side of a wooden planked boat, also called "wash strake"

sheet Line used to control a sail's lateral movement

sheet anchor Vessel's largest anchor

sheet bend A knot useful for bending a line to an eye

sheet cable Cable attached to sheet anchor

sheet chain A chain used as a cable for a sheet anchor

sheet home Pulling the sail taut while coming hard onto the wind

shelf Planks on the inside of a vessel used to support the ends of the deck beams; also called "deck shelf"

shell The case of a block

shellback An old and experienced sailor

shell ventilator A low profile air scoop

shield keel Short keel with a bulge at the bottom for added stability

shingle ballast Coarse gravel

ship Large seagoing vessel

ship biscuit Below average bread and food; also called "ship's bread" and "hardtack"

shipboard The side of a ship

ship borer Slender bivalve mollusk which bores into wooden ship bottoms and structures around the shore; also called "ship worm"

shipborne Transported or designed to be transported on a ship

ship breaker An individual who makes a business of breaking up vessels no longer suited for the sea

ship broker Person who buys and sells vessels for himself or for others in order to make a profit

shipbuilder One who designs and builds ships

ship canal A canal capable of handling sea-going vessels

ship carver Individual who carves figureheads and other ornamental items for vessels

ship chandler Merchant who deals primarily in marine equipment and supplies for a vessel

ship fever Typhus

shipfitter One who positions the structural members of a ship making ready for the welding or riveting

shipful As many or as much as a vessel can carry

shipholder Owner of a vessel

ship jack Compact and portable, hydraulic jack used to lift ships

ship keeper Watchman on a vessel while docked

shiplap Wooden sheathing in which the planks are rabbeted so that the edges of each plank, lap over the edges of the adjacent planks making a flush joint

shipless Having no ships

ship letter A letter carried by a ship not engaged in the mail service

shipload As much as the vessel will hold whether people and/or cargo

shipman Sailor, seaman

shipmaster The master or commander of a ship

shipmate A fellow sailor

shipment The act of shipping or putting anything on board a vessel for delivery by the ship to some other port

shipowner Owner or the owner of shares in a ship

shipper One who sends goods aboard a ship

shipping 1. Ships in general 2. The act of making a shipment 3. Passage on a ship

shipping articles The detailed employment contract between the Captain and the crew

ship railway Railway for removing ships from the water for repair

ship-rigged Square-rigged

ship's bells Strokes of a bell marking shipboard time, such as "eight bells"

ship's clock A clock which strikes one to eight bells every half hour along with the divisions of the ship's watches

shipshape In good order, trim, tidy

ship's papers Papers which a ship is legally required to carry

ship's stores Supplies and equipment needed for the operation and upkeep of the vessel

shipway 1. An inclined structure on which a ship is built or launched 2. A ship canal

shipworm Any of the various worm appearing creatures which destroy wooden hulls and piling by boring into them, see "ship borer"

shipwreck A ship being destroyed by grounding or floundering

shipwright A skilled carpenter in boat construction and repair

shipyard Specific area in which ships are built or repaired

shiver To shake the wind out of a sail

shoal keel Short, stubby keel, good for shallow water

shock cord An elastic cord useful for storage situations

shoe Piece of wood used for the bill of an anchor to rest upon

shoe-block Block with two sheaves, one horizontal, the other perpendicular

shore 1. The line which divides the land from the sea; the land and coast adjacent to the ocean, sea, large lake or river 2. A prop or stanchion, placed under a beam

in shore *Close to the shore*

on shore *On land or on land near the water*

shorefront A strip of land that fronts on a beach, beachfront

shoreline Strip of land where a body of water and the shore meet

shoreside Situated at or near the shore

shoreward Toward the shore

short block Replacement engine except the cylinder heads, intake manifold and carburetor from the previous engine continue to be used

short board Short tack

shorten sail Take in canvas in order to reduce the sail area

short splice A quick splice, moderately strong but bulky

short stay Is a reference to a vessel's anchor cable when it is less than one and a half times the depth of the water

short top-timber The timber above each of the second futtocks

shoulder-block A large single block having a projection on the shell to prevent the rope that is roved through it from becoming jammed between the block and the yard

shoulder of mutton sail Triangular sail used chiefly to set on a boat's mast

shrimp boat A vessel specifically rigged for shrimp fishing

shrink wrap A plastic covering put over boats while in storage or shipment. After the plastic is placed over the vessel, it is heated with a heat gun. This causes it to shrink and form a tight covering around the boat

shroud bridle An eyelet attached to the shroud in order to confine the halyard

shroud hoop Band with fittings placed around the mast to take the top of the outer shrouds, may also take the stays and tackle in which case it is called a "mast band"

shroud plates Iron bolted to side of ship, to which chains and dead-eyes of the lower rigging are connected; also called "chain plates" and "channel plates"

shrouds "Standing (fixed) rigging" from the mast to the sides of a sailboat

shut in the land Lose sight of the land by it being obscured by a point or promontory

sidelights Red and green navigation lights

side wheeler A vessel propelled by paddle wheels on the sides

Sierra Used to indicate the letter "S"

signal halyards Ropes on "signal masts" used to hoist flags

signal mast Small masts on motorboats from which flags can be flown

sills Horizontal timber between the frames to form and secure openings

single Spanish burton Tackle having three single blocks

single whip antenna Thin and relatively long fiberglass antenna with a wire inside

sink Go to the bottom

sinnit Braid formed by plaiting rope-yarns together; also called "sennit"

sisal Fiber from Indonesia and Africa which was very popular in rope making, not considered as good as "manilla"

sister block Two blocks of the same size, attached to a ring and used for jib-halyards

sister hooks Flat hooks that are designed to only connect with one another, used as a fast method to connect two lines

skeg 1. Timbers used to deepen the after part of a keel 2. A metal fitting extending back from the underside of the keel to protect the rudder and propeller

skene chock Fairlead on which the horns are angled next to one another. The rope enters and is trapped easily; also called "continental fairlead"

ski eyes Eye bolts on the stern of smaller power boats used to connect water skiing lines to the vessel

skiff A small boat which may be propelled by oars, sail or outboard motor. May be open or decked over

skin Sides of the hold

skin fitting A through-hull fitting which brings in or expels water for the galley, washbasins, toilets

skipper Informal name for owner-operator of a recreational vessel; also may be referred to as "Captain"

ski pylon Post towards the stern of a power boat to which water skiing lines can be attached. Boats designed for water skiing will normally have this instead of the more typical eye bolts on the stern

skygazer A skysail

skylark Running up and down a ship's rigging in sport

skylight Normally a hatch type opening with glass for light and ventilation

skysail Light sail next above the royal

skyscraper Triangular skysail

slabline Small line used to haul up the foot of a course

slab reefing Flaking the sail on top of the boom

slab sided 1. High sided vessel 2. When a vessel's sides run up perpendicularly from the bends; also called "wall sided"

slack The part of a rope or sail which hangs down loose

slack in stays The sail of a vessel when she works slowly in tacking

slack water Period of time between flood and ebb currents when there is no flow in either direction, not the same as "stand"

slamming Action of a vessel coming down hard while going through a headsea

slatting Slow, rhythmic beating of the sails when a ship is becalmed

sleepers Knees that connect the transoms to the after timbers on the ship's quarter

sliding keel Another name for "drop keel," a retractable keel, centerboard, dagger board

sling dog An iron hook for a sling with a fang at one end and an eye at the other for a rope, used in pairs with connecting tackle

slings 1. Large rope fitted to go around something which is to be hoisted 2. Straps used to remove smaller boats from the water by passing the "slings" under the vessel and lifting it with a crane or travel lift 3. A rope or chain attached to the middle of a lower yard and passing around a mast near the masthead used to support the yard 4. A rope net or similar object used to enclose items to be hoisted

slip A berth for a boat between two piers or floats

slip clutch Prevents damage to the engine when the propeller strikes a hard object by absorbing the force prior to reaching the engine. Smaller boats will often use a "shear pin" for the same purpose

slip dock Dock where the decking slopes towards the water, so that the lower end is in deep water and the upper end above the high water mark

slip knot Knot which will come apart when the loose end is pulled upon

slip-rope Rope bent to the cable outside of the hawse-hole. Brought in on the weather quarter when ready to slip the anchor

slips Areas out from a pier or wharf often formed by piles in which boats are berthed

slip stopper Device for suddenly releasing an anchor, chain or cable

slipstream Current of water from the propeller around the rudder

slip the cable Let the cable run out freely

slipway Inclined plane at the water's edge on which vessels are "hauled out" of the water; also called "railway" or "marine railway"

sloop Boat having a single mast, with a mainsail and a jib

slop or slops Clothes and bedding of a sailor, implies cheap and ready made clothing; name given to ready made clothing supplied by the Captain

slop chest Clothing and personal items carried on a vessel for sale to the ship's personnel

slot effect Wind speed differential from redirected wind in the area between the mainsail and the jib, an important aerodynamic effect in sailing

smack 1. A sloop or cutter rigged vessel 2. A partially decked sailing vessel used for fishing

small craft Another term for "boat"

small craft advisory Forecast indicating sea conditions dangerous to small craft operation

small craft charts Compact charts designed for use in confined areas

small stuff Cordage used primarily for whippings and servings

smoke sail Small sail raised before the funnel of a ship's galley to allow the smoke to rise before being blown aft

snake To pass small stuff across a seizing, with marling hitches at the outer turns

snap hook Hook with a spring loaded pin which prevents a line from coming out of the hook

snapper boat A commercial, "snapper" fishing vessel with hydraulic or electric reels in the stern, often being long line

snap shackle Similar to a snap hook except that the hook itself swings open to accept or release a line

snatch To place in a snatch-block

snatch block Single block with a side opening below sheave to receive the bight of a rope

snotter Rope going over the yard-arm, with an eye, used to bend the tripping-line, sending down top-gallant

snow Brig-rigged vessel with its driver (the fore-and-aft spanker sail) attached to a small mast just aft of the mainmast

snub a cable/snub a line 1. To check a running rope quickly around a cleat 2. When the line is prevented from running out any further

snubber Piece of rubber attached to and causing slack in a section of anchor chain, acts as a shock absorber

snubbing winch Winch on which the slack in the line is hand pulled in order to tighten, has no handle

snub post A short post on the deck or a landing to which a line may be fastened to check a vessel's motion; also called "snubbing post"

snying To work in the bows of a vessel

so! An order to stop hauling anything

soft chine Vessels with less angle where the bottom and the topsides of the vessel meet at a well-defined area, have a "soft" chine

soft laid A soft line due to it being laid up loosely

soldier's wind Beam wind which is the easiest course to steer, don't have to be sailor, even a soldier can steer such a course

sole Cabin or cockpit floor

SOS Morse code distress signal

sound 1. To determine the depth of the water with a lead line 2. Narrow passage of water between land and an island

sounding pole Long slender pole with depths marked off from the lower end which can be used to determine depths in shallow waters

soundings 1. Determining water depths with instruments 2. Measurement of the depth of water as shown on a chart

on-soundings *When a vessel is not too far from shore to take "soundings," normally considered to be within the 100 fathom line*

southern cross Four bright stars in the southern hemisphere, situated at the extremities of a Latin Cross and including the constellation of which these stars are the brightest

sou'wester or southwester 1. Long oilskin coat worn at sea during foul weather 2. A wide, waterproof hat with a slanting brim longer in the back than in the front

span Rope with both ends made fast, so a purchase can be hooked to its bight

Spanish burton Tackle having three blocks. A single burton uses single blocks while a double burton uses double blocks

Spanish fox Untwisting a single yarn and laying it up in an opposite manner

Spanish reef Quick but not very neat method of reefing a sail

Spanish windlass An effective method of pulling two pieces or objects together. A rope is tied in a circle around both objects, a board is inserted within the circle and turned twisting the rope together upon itself

spanker After sail of a ship or bark

spanker boom The boom which serves to extend the foot of the spanker

spanking pace Fast, exciting

spanner wrench Wrench that straddles the object to be opened. May have pins which go into holes on the object or it may be adjustable

spar buoys No longer in common use. Normally painted logs which have been trimmed, shaped and anchored by a chain

spar deck Upper deck of a vessel which gets its name because it is the deck on which spare spars are stowed

spars Masts, booms, gaffs and poles used in sailboat rigging

bend a sail *Make fast to the spar*

speak You "speak" to a vessel when communicating with another vessel at sea

speaking trumpet Trumpet used in conveying orders on board a vessel or to "speak" with another vessel

spectacles Clew iron which is shaped like a figure eight, used to attach to the clew when chain sheets are used

speed of wave Velocity of a wave at its crest, not the water which forms the wave which moves very little

spell 1. Common term for a portion of time given to any work 2. To relieve another

spencer Fore-and-aft sail (gaff-no boom) hoisted from a small mast just abaft of the fore and main masts

spencer-mast Small mast just aft of the fore and main masts, used for the "spencer" sail

spherical buoys Special purpose buoys, not used as normal aids to navigation

spherical compass Compass with a hemispherical dome over it which magnifies the compass card

spider band Collar around the mast which is fitted with belaying pins or cleats

spike bowsprit Single bowsprit used as both a bowsprit and a jib boom

spile Wooden plug normally used to seal circular screw and nail holes

spill To shake the wind out of the sails

spilling line Rope used to shake wind out of the sails

spindrift The blinding haze on salt water which is blown from the surface in a violent storm; also called "spoondrift"

spinnaker Three-cornered sail used in downwind sailing

spinnaker pole Spar used to spread the foot of the spinnaker sail, one end attaches to the mast, the other end to a clew in the sail

spinnaker pole end Fitting at each end of the spinnaker pole which has a lanyard operated clipping device in order to clip the pole to the mast and the sail

spinnaker pole mast ring Fitting on the mast to which the spinnaker pole is attached

spirit compass The modern style of compass

spitfire jib Name of a small storm jib

splash it Slang for launching a boat

splice To join two lines by interweaving the parts of the ropes

spline planking A wedge-shaped spline is glued and hammered into the seam on "carvel" built hulls to seal the seams. When the glue hardens, the excess is planed away. This is a good method of sealing a wooden boat when the seams are too wide for caulking

split backstay Backstay which is single at the mast but forks into two and secured to either side of the cockpit area

sponson Wide rubbing strip around deck level

sponsons Special planing surfaces used on hydroplane hulls

spoondrift Water swept from the top of the waves by the wind and which covers the sea's surface; also called "spindrift"

sport fisherman Normally a fast boat with special equipment used for off-shore game fishing

spray Sprinkling dashed from the top of waves by the wind

spray board Board fastened to the upper edge of the gunwale to keep out spray

spray rail An external rail just above the waterline for deflecting the spray downward

spread A sprit for extending a sail

spreader lights Flood lights attached to the mast's spreader for general illumination

spreaders Arms used to spread the shrouds and give better support to the mast

spring 1. Crack or split in a mast or yard 2. A leak, such as to "spring a leak"

spring a butt Loosen the end of a plank in a ship's bottom

spring a leak Begin to leak

spring a luff To force a vessel close to the wind when sailing

spring beam The fore-and-aft timber uniting the outer ends of the paddle-box beams

spring block A common block connected to a ringbolt by a spiral spring. It is attached to the sheets, so as to give some elasticity and to assist in sailing

spring line Dock line from the bow going aft or from the stern going forward which prevents the boat from moving fore or aft

spring-stay Horizontal stay running between mastheads of a schooner; a preventer stay used to assist the principal stay

spring tide Occurs with the full moon at which time the tide is the highest and the lowest

sprit 1. Small boom or gaff used with sails in small boats 2. Spar that crosses a fore-and-aft sail diagonally

spritsail Sail extended by a sprit

spritsail-yard Yard lashed across the bowsprit used to spread the guys of the jib

spun yarn Rope made by twisting together two or three rope-yarns

spurling line Line between the tiller and the rudder's telltale

spurling pipe Pipe through which the anchor line passes through the deck to the "chain locker"; also called "deck pipe" and "navel pipe"

spurs 1. Timber on bilge-ways which have their upper ends bolted to vessels' sides above the water 2. Curved pieces of timber used as half beams to support the deck where whole beams can not be used

spur-shoes Large pieces of timber abaft the pump-well

squall Sudden and violent windstorm

squared When yards are horizontal and at right angles with the keel

square knot Good knot for tying around an object, not the best knot for tying two lines together; also called reef knot, used to tie reef

square-rigged Vessels on which the principal sails are are four-sided and set athwartships (across)

square sail A "square-sail" is a temporary sail set at the main-mast of a sloop, when going before the wind

SRM (abbr) Speed of relative movement

stability Stiffness of a vessel

stabilizer Fins in the water to the side of a vessel that are mechanically controlled. Used to reduce the amount of roll

staff Pole or mast, used to hoist flags upon

stainless steel An alloy of iron with chromium and sometimes nickel or manganese, very corrosion resistant

stanchion 1. Supports for life rails and lines 2. Upright posts placed to support the beams of a vessel

stand When there is little or no change in the tide's water level which occurs at both high and low tides not the same as "slack tide"

stand by! A command, to be prepared to act at once

stand by Remaining with another craft to provide assistance if necessary

standing backstay The permanent aft backstay

standing part 1. Any stationary line on a tackle which does not move since it is attached to the block or to a object as compared to any line which moves and which is called the "running part" 2. The portion of a line not used in making a knot

standing rigging Permanent stays and shrouds used to hold up the mast

stand on Continue with the same course and speed

stand-on vessel The privileged vessel

starb'd Normal pronunciation for starboard

starboard Right side of the boat, pronounced "starb'd"

starboard quarters Starboard side of a vessel, from amidships to the stern

starboard tack When a sailboat has the wind coming over the starboard (right) side

starbowlines Men on the starboard watch

start You "start" a sheet when it is eased off

stateroom Private cabin which may have its own head

station bill List showing everyone's station in case of an emergency

station buoys A back-up buoy used in conjunction with a main buoy, marks location in the event the main buoy is sunk or washed away

stations Structural ribs of the vessel

statute mile Land mile (5,280 feet); nautical mile is 6,076 feet

stay To tack a vessel so that wind is brought to the other side, around the vessel's head

stayhole One of the holes in the staysail by means of which it is seized to the stay

stays Rigging used to support the masts in a fore-and-aft direction

staysail Triangular fore-and-aft sail set from a stay

stay tackle A large tackle attached to the mainstay by means of a pendant and used to hoist heavy objects such as boats

steady To keep the helm as it is

steadying sail Sail which is not for propulsion but for an easier ride in rough seas, used frequently on trawlers

steamer A ship propelled by steam

steerage That part of the between-decks which is forward of the cabin

steerageway Sufficient motion to enable a vessel to respond to the rudder

steering pulley Spring loaded pulley used in the vessel's steering system

steeve 1. The angle a bowsprit makes with the horizon 2. A heavy spar with block at one end used for stowing cargo 3. To stow cargo in a vessel's hold

stem The upright post of the bow, the extreme leading edge of the hull, on wooden boats the main structural member of the bow

stem bands Metal frequently fitted over the stem to protect it when hitting floating objects or docks

stem fitting or cap Fitting over the stem head to which the forestay may be attached, may have a bowsprit band and an anchor roller

stem head Very top of the stem

stemming Maintaining the same position despite the tide and the wind

step 1. A place in which the base of the mast is placed for support 2. To raise the mast and put it into place

stern Rear end of the boat

by the stern Drawing the most water aft, the stern of the vessel is lower than her head

down by the stern The vessel's stern draft is excessive; also called "trims by the stern"

lay aft Go to the stern of the vessel

trims by the stern Vessel's stern draft is excessive; also called "down by the stern"

stern-board When the vessel goes stern foremost

stern drive The motor is an inboard type motor mounted in the hull, the driving unit is external and similar to the lower section of an outboard engine; also called I/O, outdrive, inboard-outboard

stern fast Rope by which the stern of a vessel is secured

sternforemost Going backwards

stern frame Frame around the inside of the transom, composed of the stern post and fashion-pieces

stern light Navigation light on a vessel's stern

stern line Dock line leading aft from the stern

sternmost Farthest astern

stern post The rudder is attached to the "stern post"

stern-sheets After part of a row boat, abaft the rowers, where the passengers sit

sternson The end of the keelson to which the sternpost is attached

sternward Aft, towards the stern

sternway Moving backwards

> *fetch sternway* Making progress backward

stern wheeler A vessel propelled by a paddle wheel in the stern

stevedore A man who loads and unloads cargoes of vessels

stiff A vessel which can carry a great deal of sail without lying over on her side, opposite of crank

stirrups Ropes with thimbles at their ends, through which foot-ropes are rove and by which they are kept up towards the yards

stock Beam secured to the upper end of an anchor shank

stockless anchor Anchor without a stock which is easier to stow on the deck

stocks The frame upon which a vessel is built

stock tackle Tackle used in hoisting an anchor

stone boat Nickname given to ferro-cement boats

stools Small channels for the deadeyes of the backstays

stop a seam Caulking a seam in order to prevent a leak

stop gate A gate separating one section of a canal from another, used to shut off a section should there be a break in the embankment

stopper Stout rope with a knot at one end and sometimes a hook at the other, used for various purposes such as making fast a cable

stopper a cable To put stoppers on a cable, to prevent it from running out of the vessel when at anchor

stopper bolts Ring-bolts to which deck "stoppers" are secured

stopper knot A knot used as a stopper, made by tying a double wall knot in the line

stops Short lengths of rope used for securing various small items

stopwater Dowel driven into a bored hole to prevent leakage

storm Winds of 64 to 72 mph

storm anchor Heavy anchor used in severe winds

stormbeaten Beaten or damaged by a storm

> *ride out* To withstand the fury of a storm

storm bound Restricted to port due to the weather; also called "weather bound"

storm jib Small, strong, triangular headsail used in heavy winds

storm sail A very strong and normally smaller sized sail used in severe winds

storm stay A stay on which the "storm sail" is bent

storm wave A very high, rolling wave caused by high winds

stormwind High winds accompanying a severe storm

stove When a vessel's hull is smashed in

stow 1. Pack the cargo 2. Put something away in its proper place

stowaway A person who hides aboard a vessel in order to obtain free passage

stowed in bulk Stowed loose

straining screw A rigging screw, one end on a swivel, the other end threaded

strait Narrow passage of water between two seas or oceans, such as the Straits of Gibraltar

strake Planks running fore and aft on the outside of a vessel; also called "streak"

strand 1. A number of rope-yarns twisted together 2. Land bordering a body of water

stranded When a vessel is aground near the shore; also called "ashore"

strand line A shore line above the present water level

strap Rope or iron around a block to keep its parts together

strapped in When a vessel is hard on the wind with its sails in as far as possible

streak Planks running fore and aft on the outside of a vessel; also called "strake"

stream A steady current in a body of water, such as the Gulf Stream

stream a buoy Dropping a buoy into the water before letting go the anchor

stream anchor Used for warping, smaller than bowers, larger than kedges; also used as lighter anchor to moor by with a hawser

stream cable Lighter weight hawser that holds the stream anchor which is used in a sheltered location

stretchers Wood placed across a boat's inside bottom, for rowers to press feet against; also called "footboards"

strike Lower sail or colors

strike sail To lower the sails suddenly

stringers Longitudinal planking on the inside of the ribs adding to the hull's strength

strip To dismantle

strip planking Method of hull construction where the strakes are placed on top of the previous one and nailed downwards to it

strong breeze A wind of 25 to 31 mph

strong gale Wind having a speed of 47 to 54 mph

strop Rope secured around a spar to which blocks may be shackled

strum box Perforated box placed over the end of a suction line, such as that for the bilge pump, which filters out non-fluid items

struts External supports for the propeller shaft

stud link Normal chain link which is further strengthened with a stud across the link; looks similar to a figure eight

studding sails Light sails set outside the square sails, on booms rigged out for that purpose

stuffing box Through-hull fitting for the drive shaft or rudder post; also called a "gland." Prevents water from leaking into boat

sued Condition of a ship when she is high and dry on shore; same as "sewed"

suit of sails Sailboat's complete set of sails

sumlog Speed and distance device attached to the outside of the hull, may be an impellor or an electronic pressure switch

sun deck Normally the upper deck of a ship which is exposed to the most sun

sun dog A small halo-like bright light, sometimes tinged with rainbow colors appearing near the sun. Older mariners feel it indicates a change of weather within 48 hours

sun lights Angle between the sun and the earth's horizon as taken with a sextant

supercharger Device which forces additional air into an engine to increase the compression and the rate of firing

supporters Knee-timbers under the cat-heads

surf Waves breaking on shore, reef, bar

surge A large, swelling wave

surge the capstan Slacken the line around the capstan

surveyor Professional who examines the condition of boats for insurance or prior to purchase

survival suit A brightly colored, water immersion suit made from a rubberized fabric, insulated, containing flotation material and locating devices

SW (abbr) Southwest

swab Mop

swabs When one "mops"

swage A method of attaching an eye or jaw to the end of a rigging wire without splicing. A tube which is attached to the eye or jaw is placed over the wire and compressed onto it

swallow Opening in a common block between the block and sheave (grooved wheel) through which the line is rove

swamp To fill with water

sway To hoist up, as in hoisting the yards

sweep Large oars, used in small vessels to force them ahead

sweep of the tiller A circular frame on which the tiller travels on a large ship

sweep the deck To carry away everything movable on a deck, as by a wave

swell Long, large wave that does not crest

swift To bring two shrouds close together by ropes

swifter 1. Forward shroud to a lower mast 2. To tighten, as shrouds, by tackles 3. A rope used to confine the bars of the capstan in their sockets while men are turning it 4. A rope used to encircle a boat longitudinally in order to strengthen her sides

swig 1. A tackle with ropes which are not parallel 2. To make taut, such as a tackle, by successively pulling the fall and taking the slack around a cleat

swimming ladder Similar to a boarding ladder except that it extends down into the water

swimming platform A shelf fitted to the vessel's stern just above the waterline

swinging the compass Method of determining the compass error by swinging the vessel in a circle and stopping approximately every 10 degrees to take a compass bearing on a known fixed object. This will indicate errors on any particular heading; also called "swinging ship"

swivel block Any type of block which has a swivel for its base

swivel A twisting link used to keep turns out of a chain

SWL (abbr) Safe working load, the load limit at which any tackle may be used safely

syphering Lapping the edges of planks over each other for a bulkhead

TANGO
T

tabernacle 1. Frame used to support the foot of a mast 2. A fitting which holds but acts as a hinge in lowering the mast

tabling 1. Letting one beam-piece into another 2. A broad hem on a sail's border to which the bolt-rope is sewed

tachometer Instrument which indicates the engine's RPM (revolutions per minute)

tack 1. A sailing maneuver in which the direction of the boat is changed 2. When a sailboat heads into the wind and changes the side over which the wind blows 3. Each leg of a a zigzag course sailed 4. The tack rope attached to and the part of the sail the rope is attached to; the foremost lower corner of the courses

> *board a tack* To pull down the tack of a course to the deck of the vessel
>
> *hold tack* To last or hold out, continuing the present course
>
> *in irons* Sailboat that loses headway and stalls while coming about due to the wind being directly ahead
>
> *in stays* When a vessel is going from one tack to another; also called "hove in stays"
>
> *lay a course* A sailboat "lays her course" when she can reach her destination without tacking

tack block Block for the tack of a sail

tack of a flag A line spliced into the eye at the bottom of the tabling for securing the flag to the halyards

tack rag Slightly sticky cloth used to remove dust and dirt from a surface before it is varnished or painted

tackle Block and tackle used for mechanical advantage, a purchase

rack a tackle To bind together two ropes of a tackle to prevent the ropes from reeving back through the blocks

stock tackle Tackle used in hoisting an anchor

under run a tackle Separating the parts of a tackle and putting them in order

tackle block Block or pulley over which a rope runs

tackle fall Rope from the end of a pulley on which it is pulled

tackle hook Hook which connects the tackle to the object to be moved

tackling Anything used as tackle or any part of tackle

taffrail Rail around the ship's stern

taffrail log A speed log attached to the taffrail of the vessel

tail-block Rope spliced into the end of a block used for making it fast to rigging or spars

tail board Ornamental carved boards extending back from the bowsprit on the bow of a vessel, not to be confused with "trail boards"

tail-down stream While at anchor, the vessel's stern swings "down" with the tide

tailing Keeping a steady pressure on the line coming off a winch

tail on Take hold of a rope and pull

tail-tackle A watch tackle

tail-up stream While at anchor, the vessel's stern swings up with the tide

take a strain When all the slack in a line is pulled in and an individual begins to exert pressure on the line

take a turn Passing a rope around a pin or kevel, to keep it fast; also called a "turn"

take bearings Determine one's position by sightings with a compass

take departure You "take departure" from a known position to commence "dead reckoning"

take in Lower the sails

take in the slack To pull taut the slack part of a rope

take or have the wind To get to the windward thus gaining an advantageous position

take the wind out of one's sails To deprive another vessel of the wind by going close to the windward

take up When the planks swell from being placed in water, the seams "take up" and become watertight

tang The part at the top of the mast which takes the shroud or stay end

Tango Used to indicate the letter "T"

tar A liquid gum from pine trees used for caulking

tarpaulin Canvas used for covering hatches, boats and the like

taut Tight, snug

tee bollard Bollard shaped like the letter "T"

tee cleat Cleat shaped like the letter "T"

telltale 1. Compass hanging from the beams of a cabin so a heading can always be known 2. An instrument attached to the steering indicating the position of the rudder 3. A wind direction indicator mounted in the rigging

temperature gauge Indicates whether an engine is operating at safe temperature levels

tend To watch a vessel at anchor at the turn of tides

tender Small boat from a yacht, a dinghy

tenon The heel of the mast, made to fit into the step

tensile strength of rope Load in pounds of pull at which a rope will break

thick-and-thin block Block with one sheave larger than the other

thimble Metal fitting used in rigging, forming a reinforced place of attachment

thole pins Pair of vertical pins set in the gunwales of a rowboat (today we normally use rowlocks)

throat 1. Forward upper corner of a four-sided fore-and-aft sail 2. That part of the oar where the "loom" (shaft) becomes the blade; also called the "neck"

throat halyard Halyard and blocks used in hoisting the throat end of the gaff aloft

through fastenings Bolts that go all the way through the hull or base timbers and secured with a washer and nut on the inside

through-hull fitting Fitting where water is taken in or discharged through the hull for engine cooling, waste disposal and the like

thrum Sticking short strands of yarn through a mat or canvas to make a rough surface

thrust Force exerted endwise through a propeller shaft to give forward motion. Achieved by the propeller drawing in water from ahead and pushing it out astern

thumb cleat Cleat with only one horn, used as a fairlead and lashing point

thwart A crossway seat, usually contributing to the strength of small open boat, upon which oarsmen sit

tidal 1. Of or pertaining to the rising and falling of tides 2. Depending on or regulating something happening, such as sailing, on the tides

tidal basin A basin in which the tide ebbs and flows

tidal current Horizontal flow of water accompanying the changing tides

tidal wave An unusually high wave often caused by an earthquake; alongshore it may be caused by high winds

tide Properly, it means only the rise and fall; the vertical movement of tidal waters. Common usage has extended the meaning to include "tidal current"

flood tide *Rising tide as opposed to an ebb tide*

weather tide *A tide running against the wind*

work double tides *To perform three days work in two*

tide day or tidal day Time between two successive tides at a specific location

tide-down To work down a river or harbor with the tide and anchor when the tide turns

tide gate 1. An area where the tide moves with great velocity 2. A gate at a basin through which water flows and which is closed on the ebb to prevent the water from flowing out

tideland Land bordering the sea which is alternately covered by water or exposed depending on the tide

tideless Water having no tide

tide lock A lock situated between the tidewater of a harbor and an enclosed basin when the levels vary. It has double gates by which vessels can pass either way at all times of a tide

tide rip A ripple on the surface of the sea produced by the passage of the tide over an uneven bottom but can also be caused by eddies or opposing currents

tide-rode When a vessel at anchor swings with the tide

tide table A table indicating the time of high and low tides at a specific location throughout the year

tide-up To work up a river or harbor with the tide and anchor when the tide turns

tidewater Coastal regions in which the water level is subject to tidal action

tide wave Same as tidal wave

tideway A channel in which the tide sets

tier The range of fakes of a cable or hawser

tiller A lever attached to the rudder post which is used to steer the vessel

sweep of the tiller *A circular frame on which the tiller travels on a large ship*

tiller chain A chain leading from the tiller-head around the barrel of the wheel by which the vessel is steered

tiller extension Rod attached to the tiller which allows the helmsman a greater area from which to steer, useful in sailboat races when the helmsman may wish to lean out over the side

tiller extension universal Coupling between the tiller and the extension

tiller head The extremity of the tiller to which the tiller rope or chain is attached

tiller rope 1. A rope which answers the purpose or a tiller chain 2. In small craft, a rope extending to each side of the deck from the tiller-head, used to aid the helmsman in controlling the helm in a strong breeze

timber General term for all large pieces of wood

floor timber *A timber placed immediately across the keel*

timber-head Top end of a timber which rises above the gunwale, used for belaying lines

timber hitch The end of the rope taken around a spar, led under and over the standing part and passed two or three turns around its own part

time charter Chartering a vessel with a crew

tingle A temporary patch over a leak

tip Outer end of the oar's blade, sometimes it is metal-sheathed to reduce wear

to windward Sailing into the wind with it as far ahead as possible; also called "on the wind," "close hauled" or "beating"

toe rail 1. Low bulwark on a small decked boat 2. Narrow strips placed on top of the gunwale which finishes it off and provides some safety for those on the deck

toe rail capping Ornamental strip laid on top of the toe rail

toe straps Straps running along the bottom of a skiff used as a foot hold for the crew when leaning out

toggle A pin placed through the eye of a bolt, to keep it in its place

tonnage Measure of capacity or displacement

top Platform placed over the head of a lower mast

top-block A strong block, under the lower cap, used for the top-rope to reeve through in order to send up and down the topmasts

topgallant mast Third mast above the deck

topgallant sail Third sail above the deck

top light A signal lantern carried to the top

top-lining Lining on the after part of sails to prevent chafing against the top-rim

topman or topsman Mariner whose station is in the top

topmast Second mast above the deck

topmast-head The top of the topmast

top pendant A rope by which the topmasts are hoisted or lowered

topping The act of pulling one ex-tremity of a yard or boom higher than the other

topping lift Running rigging line used to control a spar

top-rope Rope used for sending topmasts up and down

topsail Second sail above the deck

rolling topsail A topsail which may be taken in around a roller under the sail

double topsails Two sails on a square-rigged vessel corresponding in width to the topsail formally carried on a square-rigger but only half as high. The upper sail has a yard which may be hoisted or lowered but the yard of the lower sail is stationary

topsail schooner Schooner rigged vessel carrying square sails on the foremast

topsail yard Yard to which the topsail is bent

topsides 1. On deck 2. The side skin of a boat between the waterline and the deck

top tackle A large tackle hooked to the lower end of the topmast top-rope and to the deck

top timbers Highest timbers on a vessel's side

long top-timber The timber above each of the first futtocks

short top-timber The timber above each of the second futtocks

toss To throw an oar out of its oarlock, raise it perpendicularly and lay it in the boat with the blade forward

touch A sail is said to "touch," when the wind strikes the leech and shakes it a little

toward the wind A vessel changes course "toward the wind"

towboat A tugboat designed for towing but may also push other vessels

towing Pulling a vessel through the water

track 1. Path that a vessel is expected to follow, normally shown on a chart 2. A track on the mast in which the sail's track slides are fastened

track slides Connect the sail to the sail track

traffic separation scheme A plan for congested areas where vessels use one-way lanes

trail boards Ornamental board on each side of the stem and stretching from it forward to the figurehead

transit A line between an observer and two objects which are in line

transom 1. Flat area across the stern 2. Timbers across and bolted to the stern post 3. Raised platforms in smaller vessels used as seats

transom handle A small carrying handle attached to small boats

transom-knees Knees which are bolted to the transoms and after timbers

trapeze A line from the mast with a harness for a crewman at the end; allows a crewman to hang out over the side

trapeze ring Connects the "trapeze" line to the harness and provides a handhold for the crewman

traveler 1. Crosspiece, athwartships on sailboat's cabin top, cockpit or transom to which the mainsail's boom is fastened. Used to control the angle of the mainsail without a mainsheet 2. Iron ring fitted so as to slip up and down the rigging

travel lift Mobile equipment with slings used to remove vessels from the water and transport them short distances

trawl A large conical net dragged along the ocean's bottom in order to catch fish

trawler 1. A boat used in trawl fishing 2. A person who fishes by trawling 3. Deep draft, displacement type vessel. Current recreational vessels using this name tend to be look-alikes

trawlerman A fisherman who uses a trawl or crews on a trawler

treenails Long wooden pins, used for nailing a plank to a timber; also called "trunnels" and "trenail"

trend The lower end of the shank of an anchor

trestle-trees Two timbers, placed horizontally and fore-and-aft on opposite sides of the masthead

triatic stay A stay which connects two masts together

trice To haul up by means of a rope

trick Time allotted to a person to man the helm

trim 1. Way in which a vessel floats 2. Setting and adjusting the sails and rigging

>   *out of trim* *when a vessel's cargo is not stowed in such a way as to balance the vessel evenly*

trimaran Vessel with three hulls, a main center hull and two smaller outboard hulls

trim of masts Their position in regard to the vessel and to each other

trim of sails The position and arrangement of sails best suited for a particular vessel in propelling it forward

trims by the head Vessel is too heavily loaded forward, same as "down by the bow"

trims by the stern Vessel's stern draft is excessive; also called "down by the stern"

trim tabs Adjustable planing surface used to alter the planing attitude of the vessel

trip To raise an anchor clear of the bottom

trip line Line on an anchor used to haul it out when it is dug too deep or fouled

tripping line Line used for tripping a spar in sending it down

trough Depression in the water between two waves

truck Circular piece of wood at the head of the masts for signal halyards

true course A course in relation to "true north"

true north Actual north which will vary some from the compass "magnetic north"

true wind Actual direction and force of the wind (see "apparent wind")

trunk cabin Extends above the main deck level but allows for walkways on either side

trunk cabin cruiser Vessel with a "trunk cabin"

trunnels Long wooden pins, used for nailing a plank to a timber; also called "treenails"

truss Rope by which the center of a lower yard is kept in toward the mast

trysail A "spencer" sail

tubular jamb cleat Cleat with a tube as the top. The tube has a partial slot at the top. When line is rove through the tube it acts as a fairlead but by pulling the line up into slot, the line will jamb

tuck Where the after part of the hull rises and becomes the counter

tug boat Strongly built and powerful boat used primarily for towing and pushing other vessels; also called a "towboat"

day tug Used for short hauls, have no living accommodations

lugger tug Tug boat designed for towing with a hawser

model bow tug Typical tug with a pointed bow used primarily in towing

ocean-going tug Normally a deep draft vessel designed to operate hundreds of miles from the coast. Often will have only one propeller for fuel economy

pusher tug A tug boat designed with a blunt bow used primarily in pushing barges and other vessels; may be called "push boat"

towboat A tugboat designed for towing but often used in pushing other vessels

utility tug General purpose tug boat often used in dredging operations, moving pipe lines and personnel

coastal tug Although often capable of operating over large areas they are not normally deep draft vessels. This restricts them from safely being operated long distances from the shore. They will normally have twin propellers

tularit splice An eye formed by looping the end of a wire and then clamping a metal collar around both sections

tumblehome Inward curving of the ship's topsides, above the waterline, opposite of "wall sided"; also called "tumbling home"

tune Adjusting the sail or engine for maximum efficiency

Turks head An ornamental knot

turn Passing a rope around a pin or kevel in order to keep it fast

turnbuckle Metal sleeve with bolts entering each end and with the bolts threaded in opposite directions. When the sleeve is turned, the attached lines can be tightened or loosened

turn button A simple device, usually made from a small, oblong piece of wood with a screw holding it in place at its center. When turned over the side of a door or drawer it will hold them closed

turning block Block which turns any line from and to a fixed point

turning circle Smallest possible circle a vessel can make when the rudder is hard over

turn of the bilge Lower outer part of the hull where the sides meet the bottom

turn turtle To capsize

twin backstays Two individual backstays from the mast to either side of the stern

twin cable steering Normally used with an outboard engine. Uses two cables which allows both cables to share the pull and provides an additional measure of safety

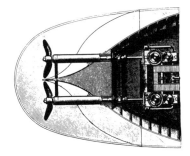

twin engine Boats with two engines and two propellers

twine Small stuff, light line used for whippings or servings

two-blocked 1. When both blocks of a purchase are drawn together and are too close to hoist any higher, same as "chock-a-block" and "two blocks" 2. When flags are fully hoisted up a signal mast

two-fold purchase Purchase using two double sheave hook-blocks; also called "double tackle"

two half-hitches Hitches are made upon the line and then tightened, a useful knot

two part paints Yacht finishes which require the two parts be mixed by the user. This causes a chemical reaction and a better finish

two shot method When ferrocement construction is a two step process. Half the hull thickness is plastered from the outside and then half from the inside

tye Rope connected with a yard, the other end is attached to a tackle for hoisting

typhoon High intensity, tropical revolving storm in the Pacific

UNIFORM
U

UHF (abbr) Ultra high frequency (radio)

UL (abbr) Underwriters Laboratories, a testing organization that helps set safety standards

unbend Cast off

under canvas Under sail

under canvassed Not carrying enough sail for the conditions

under gun'l rod racks Racks in the cockpit area of smaller boats which provide a storage place for fishing rods under the gun'l

undermasted A vessel with masts of less than the usual dimensions

under run To pass under in a boat

under run a tackle Separating the parts of a tackle and putting them in order

under sail With the sails spread

under sparred Does not have sufficient spars

under the lee On the side sheltered from the wind, when something is between the vessel and the wind

underway When a vessel moves through the water, having weighed anchor and making progress

underway with no way on Adrift

Underwriters Laboratories A testing organization, that helps set safety standards (abbr UL)

unfurl Freeing the sails in preparation of hoisting

Uniform Used to indicate the letter "U"

union Upper portion of the flag near the hoist, the blue area with the stars on the U. S. flag

union-down Flying the Union upside down, used as a distress signal

union jack Flag consisting of only the union of the national flag

unlaying Line which is untwisting

unmoor To heave up one anchor so the vessel may ride at a single anchor

unship To remove something from where it is fixed such as to "unship the rudder"

unstep Removing the mast from the mast "step"

upper shrouds Shrouds attached to the top of the mast

upper works The part of a ship above the water when fully loaded or in ballast; also called "dead works"

upside-down tornado Mass of rapidly shifting, cold air spilling down from thunderstorm clouds at very high speeds; also called "microburst"

upwind To the windward of

USCG (abbr) U.S. Coast Guard

USN (abbr) U.S. Navy

USPS (abbr) United States Power Squadrons

utility boat Normally considered a boat that is used for work purposes

utility tug boat General purpose tug boat often used in dredging operations, moving pipelines and personnel

VICTOR

V-berth Any sleeping compartment in the "fo'-c's'l"

V-drive Permits the engine to be mounted very close to the stern. The drive shaft goes forward to a gear box instead of aft, then reverses its direction

vane A fly at the mast-head to show wind direction

vane steering Various designs available, basically a small rudder that is attached to the main rudder and which is controlled by a wind vane

vang Rope leading from the peak of the gaff of a fore-and-aft sail to the rail on each side, used to steady the gaff

variation A compass "error," a variation from "true north"

varnish Contains oil, resin, solvent, driers and additives, including ultraviolet additives

vector A line drawn to represent the effect of wind and current

vee bottom One of the three basic bottom shapes—flat, round and vee

veer 1. To swerve 2. To "veer out" is to let out line 3. Wind veers when it changes direction

veer and haul To haul and slack until a vessel gets underway

veer out the cable To lessen the strain on a line and let it out slowly; also said "ease a line" and "pay out"

ventilator Any device that allows fresh air to enter below decks, quite a number of designs available

venturi A pumping system which uses the force of passing water in order to operate, such as the "self bailer" in a speed boat

very lights A pyrotechnic distress signal fired by a special pistol

very pistol Pistol which fires "very lights"

vessel Any moving and floating craft

VHF (abbr) Very high frequency (radio)

Victor Used to indicate the letter "V"

viol A larger messenger used in weighing an anchor by a capstan; also the block through which the messenger passes

VLF Very low frequency (radio)

voltage regulator Flow of electricity from the engine's generator or alternator goes through this device which prevents the batteries from being overcharged

voltmeter Monitors the condition of the electrical charging system and the state of the batteries

voyage A complete trip

WHISKEY

W

W Used to indicate the compass setting of "West"

wad punch Punch used to make holes for a metal eyelet in leather, canvas or synthetic materials

waist Upper deck between the quarter-deck and the forecastle

waist anchor An anchor carried in the waist of a vessel; a sheet anchor

waist boat A boat stowed and carried in the waist of a vessel; on whalers this is the boat commanded by the second mate

waist boater One who commands the waist boat

waist cloth The hammock coverings of the waist-nettings

waisters Green hands, term comes from when they were placed in the waist of a man-of-war

wake Disturbed water astern of a vessel caused by her passage

wales Strong planks in the vessel's side running her entire length

wall Knot put on the end of a rope

wall sided 1. High sided vessel 2. When a vessel's sides run up perpendicularly from the bends; also called "slab sided"

waning The moon in its third and fourth quarter when the illumination is decreasing

ward room Room in which commissioned officers live

ware Same result as tacking except

the vessel's stern is carried around by the wind

warp To move a vessel by means of a rope made fast to some fixed object

wash 1. Broken water left behind a vessel as it moves along 2. Flow of water caused by a vessel's propellers

wash-board Light pieces of board placed above a gunwale of a boat

wash strake Topmost plank on the side of a wooden planked boat; also called "sheer strake"

watch 1. A division of time on board a ship 2. A buoy is said to "watch," when it floats upon the surface

rotate the watch Changing the persons on "watch"

watch-and-watch Term for a four hour watch

watch ho! Cry of the man that heaves the deep-sea-lead

watch tackle Small luff purchase, short fall, double block with hook and tail, for deck use

waterage The cost of transporting by water

waterboard A board fastened to the weather side of a vessel to keep the spray out

watercourse Natural or man made channel through which water flows

watercraft 1. Craft for water transport 2. Skill in managing a vessel

water dog A skilled sailor who is quite at ease on the water

waterfront Land or a section of a community fronting on a body of water

watergall A rainbow colored spot appearing in the sky which indicates to those with experience a forecast of rain; also called a "weather gall"

waterlight An electric light attached to a life ring, often automatically operated, used for man-overboard accidents at night

waterline 1. Any of several lines which may be marked on the outside of a vessel and which correspond with the water's surface when the vessel is floating evenly 2. Intersection of the hull and the water's surface

length on the waterline *vessel length measured along the waterline; also called "load waterline"*

water-logged When a vessel takes on so much water that she becomes unmanageable by the helm and at the mercy of the waves

waterman 1. Man who works mostly on or near the water. 2. A boatman for hire

watermanship The business, skill or art of a waterman; oarsmanship

water pressure pump Provides pressurized water in the vessel's plumbing system

water pressure regulator Reduces high water pressures from marina hookups to pressure compatible with the vessel's plumbing system

water pump Circulates water for the cooling of the engine

water rat 1. A waterfront loafer or petty thief 2. Slang for children who spend hours on or in the water

water right Riparian right

water-sail A save-all sail, set under the swinging-boom

waterside Margin or bank along a body of water; waterfront

waterspout A funnel-shaped column of rotating cloud-filled wind normally extending down to the surface of the water, similar to the land-based tornado,

watertight So tight as to retain or not admit water

watertight bulkheads Leak-proof walls with or without watertight doors

waterways 1. Fore-and-aft timbers connecting the deck with the sides, the scuppers run through them 2. A channel 3. Navigable body of water

waves Vertical movement of water regardless of forward motion

way Movement of a vessel through the water

ways Inclined planes at the water's edge on which vessels are "hauled out" of the water; also called "marine ways" or "railways"

wear or wearing ship To bring the vessel on another tack by turning the ship's stern through the wind; also called "doing an old man"

weather In the direction from which the wind blows

weather beam Direction to the windward, at right angles to the keel

weather-bitt Taking an extra turn of the cable about the end of the bitt or the windlass-end

weatherboard 1. That side of the vessel which is toward the wind, the weather side of a vessel 2. A board inclined near a porthole in order to keep the water but not the air out

weather-bound Restricted to port due to the weather; also called "storm bound"

weathercloth Long piece of canvas or a tarpaulin used to preserve hammocks for injury when stowed along the quarter rails on older ships

weather deck Deck without overhead protection from the weather

weather dog A broken or fragmentary rainbow believed by seamen to forecast rain

weather eye Ability of a person being able to quickly observe coming changes in the weather

weather-gage A vessel has the "weather-gage" of another ship when she is windward of her

weather-gall A secondary rainbow said to be a sign of bad weather, a "water-gall"

weatherglass Simple glass instrument which shows changes in atmospheric pressure by the water level changing in its spout

weather helm Tendency of a vessel to turn to the windward requiring little helm. This is normally considered a safety element in a sailboat's design

weatherly ship Ship that works well to the windward

weather quarter The quarter of the vessel on which the wind blows

weather-roll Roll which a ship makes to windward

weather ship A ship which makes routine weather observations

weather shore When a vessel finds shelter from the wind in the "lee" of the land

weather side Side of the vessel upon which the wind is blowing

weather tide The tide which sets against the lee side of a vessel, pushing her to the windward; a tide running against the wind

weather-wise A person who is skillful in forecasting changes in the weather

weigh To raise the anchor

well-found A ship which is well supplied and fitted out

westing A westward passage, going westward

wetted surface The area of a vessel in the water which affects a vessel's speed

whaleback A steamer or barge with a convex upper deck, at one time used on the Great Lakes

whaleboat or whaler 1. Long narrow rowboat, sharp at both ends, formally used for whaling 2. A modern day version of this boat is propelled by oars or a motor

whale built A vessel built along the lines of a "whaleboat"

whale fishery 1. Fishing for whales 2. That part of the ocean where whale fishing is carried on

whaler 1. Vessel or individuals engaged in whale fishing 2. A whaleboat

whaling Whale fishing

wharf Structure, parallel to shore, used for docking

wharfage 1. The wharf facilities 2. Charge for using the wharf 3. Use of the wharf 4. Handling and stowing of goods on a wharf

wharf boat A kind of boat moored in a river which is used as a floating dock

wharfing 1. Wharves in general 2. Material for wharves

wharfinger Person who owns or manages a wharf

wharfman Man employed to work on a wharf

wharfmaster Manager of a wharf

wharf rat Individual who loafs around a wharf and may be a common thief

wheel Steering wheel, occasionally used to refer to the propeller

wheel chain A chain used to connect the wheel and the rudder which operates the same as a "wheel rope"

wheelhouse Pilothouse; a shelter for the helmsman

wheelman or wheelsman The helmsman

wheel rope Rope reeved through a block on each side of the deck and led around the barrel of the steering wheel, to assist in steering

whip 1. A purchase formed by a rope rove through a single block 2. Name often given to the basic VHF antenna, normally fiberglass with the wire inside

whipped Wrapping twine or thread around a line to add strength and prevent it from untwisting; also called "seized" or "whipping"

whisker poles Pole between the mast and the clew that serves to hold the clew of the head sail or jib out to the side on a downwind run

whiskers Cross-trees to a bowsprit

Whiskey Used to indicate the letter "W"

whistle buoys Use compressed air produced by the sea's motion to sound a whistle

whistle signal Standard form of communication between boats, may be used to indicate danger, change of course and other situations

whitecaps Foam on top of waves; the crest of a wave

white horses Fast moving white capped waves

whole gale Wind having a speed of 55 to 63 mph

wide "dee" shackles Shackles with wider than normal jaws

winch Mechanical device used to increase the pull on a line or chain

   self tailing winch Line coming off the winch is secured through a type of a cam cleat which prevents the line from slipping back

wind Direction and force of wind relative to the moving vessel

   away from the wind When a sailboat's bow moves downwind, a vessel changes course "away from the wind"

   before the wind Wind is coming from the aft

   by the wind Vessel is sailing as close into the wind as possible; also called "close hauled," "on the wind," "to windward" or "beating"

   haul her wind When a vessel comes up close upon the wind

   have a free wind To be able to sail free

   how the wind blows or lies The direction or velocity of the wind

   in the teeth of the wind Same as to "sail in the wind's eye"

   in the wind's eye To sail directly into the wind; same as "in the teeth of the wind"

   off the wind Sailing free with the yard eased off

   on the wind Sailing close to the wind, close-hauled

   sail close to the wind Sailing with the vessel's head so near to the wind as to fill the sails without shaking them

   shake a vessel in the wind To luff a vessel until her upper sails shake

   soldier's wind Beam wind which is the easiest course to steer, don't have to be sailor, even a soldier can steer such a course

   take or have the wind To get to the windward thus gaining an advantageous position

   take the wind out of one's sails To deprive another vessel of the wind by going close to the windward

   toward the wind A vessel changes course "toward the wind"

wind a ship To turn it end for end, so that the wind strikes it on the opposite side

windbound When a vessel can not sail due to a contrary wind

wind dog A fragment of a rainbow seen on detached clouds regarded by older mariners as a sign of high winds

wind gauge An anemometer, an instrument showing the velocity of the wind

winding tackle Tackle consisting of one fixed triple block and one double or triple movable block, used to hoist particularly heavy loads

windjammer Nickname for a sailing vessel but normally applies to larger vessels

windlass Special form of winch with a rotating drum for hauling a line

wind rode Riding with the wind instead of to the current

wind rose Diagram showing the relative frequency or frequency and strength of winds from different directions

wind sail Specially designed canvas which hangs over an open hatch an directs the wind into the hatch

windscreen A windshield

wind shadow Wind immediately to the lee of the sail or other object which is confused and non-directional; also called "dirty wind"

windward Direction from which the wind is blowing

wing That part of the hold which is next to the sides

wing-and-wing When a vessel is dead ahead of the wind with her main sail on one side and her foresail on the other side

wingers Casks stowed in the wings of a vessel

wing keel Keel is more shallow than normal with a lead wing at the base for stability

winterizing Preparing a boat for winter by "pickling" all systems carrying fresh or salt water

withe Iron band with a ring fitted on the end of a mast through which another mast is made fast; also called "wythe"

woold To wind a piece of rope around a spar

work A vessel is said to "work" when rigid members of the construction loosen up

workboat A boat used for work purposes rather than for pleasure or passenger service. Normally, a small boat used for ferrying stores, putting down moorings and the like

work double tides To perform three days work in two

working anchor Vessel's anchor which is used in normal anchoring situations

working sails Sails used in normal winds

work one's passage Paying for passage by doing duty aboard a vessel

works A vessel "works" to the windward when gaining ground by tacks

work-up Phrase for keeping a crew constantly and needlessly at work

worm To fill in the spaces in laid rope

worm shoe An extra timber fastened externally to the bottom of the keel in order to protect it; also called a "false keel"

wring To bend a mast by setting the rigging up too taut

wring-bolts Bolts that secure the planks to the timbers

wring-staves Strong pieces of plank used with wring-bolts

wythe Iron band with a ring fitted on the end of a mast through which another mast is made fast; also called "withe"

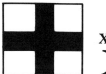

XRAY

X

Xray Used to indicate the letter "X"

YANKEE

Y

yacht A power or sailing vessel used for recreation, may be luxurious, normally over 40 feet. There is, however, no established definition

yacht basin Protected area offering the various facilities required or desirable for recreational boats; also called a "marina"

yacht built Built like a yacht

yacht club Club organized to promote and regulate boating, often provides the opportunity for competitive racing and a social setting

yachter One who sails a yacht, a yachtsman

yachting Racing or cruising in a yacht

yachtsmanship Art or science of sailing or managing a yacht

yachtsmen Owner-operators of recreational craft; also may be called "boatmen" depending on the size of the boat, no established distinction on size of the vessel

Yankee Used to indicate the letter "Y"

yard 1. A spar, crossing the mast, on which square sails are fitted 2. A boat-yard where boats are stored and repaired

　head yard *One of the yards of a vessel's foremast*

yardarm Extremities of a yard

yardarm and yardarm When the yard-arms of two, side by side vessels touch or cross

yard rope A rope passing through a block at a masthead used to hoist or lower a yard

yard sling A short chain from the middle of a lower yard to a lower masthead to aid in supporting the yard

yard tackle Tackle extending from the end of a lower yardarm used for lifting boats and various other items

yarn Material from which the individual strands of rope are made

yaw 1. To swing or steer off course 2. When a boat runs off course to the side when struck by a following sea (see "broach")

yawl Popular rig for pleasure sailboats, has two masts, the after mast is much smaller and stepped behind the rudder post

yawl rigged Rigged like a yawl

Yellow flag The quarantine flag

yeoman Person in charge of the store room

yoke Wood placed across the head of the rudder with a rope attached to each end, by which boat is steered

ZULU

Z

Z-twist Term for right-hand-lay rope

zenith A point in the heavens vertically above the observer

zephyr A breeze from the west, a gentle breeze

Zulu Used to indicate the letter "Z"